VOLUNTEERS

HOW TO GET THEM
HOW TO KEEP THEM

Helen Little

 Panacea Press, Inc.

Naperville, Illinois

 PANACEA PRESS, INC.

P.O. Box 4054, Naperville, IL   60567
Toll Free: 1-877-870-6603
Phone: 1-630-579-6603   Fax: 1-630-579-6643
Web site: www.panaceapress.com
E-mail: info@panaceapress.com

Printed in the U.S.A.
10

Library of Congress Catalog Card Number: 99-74301
ISBN-10: 1-928892-01-9
ISBN-13: 978-1-928892-01-4

This is for my family: Lynn, Craig, Eric, and Sonia for their never-ending support and encouragement.

Acknowledgments

I wish to acknowledge and thank the many people who helped with this book:

The volunteers and staff, who shared their ideas and experiences with me.

Ellen Bergschneider, who provided corrections, comments, and encouragement for the many versions of the manuscript.

Elizabeth Allan, Patricia Forbis, Geraldine Esposito, Phyllis Santos, Nancy Jordan, Gene Ruoff, Nina Hazzouri, Sandy Crane, Bill Rabior, Sue Rabior, Diane Bergschneider, Darla Smith, Kathryn Rawlings, Sandy Crowley Schwartz, and Mary Hanson, who read the manuscript and made valuable suggestions.

My sincere thanks to each of you.

Table of Contents

INTRODUCTION 1

CHAPTER ONE

The Volunteer Shortage: Myth or Reality 5

CHAPTER TWO

Setting the Stage 11

    Managing Volunteers' Expectations 13

    Managing Your Expectations 14

CHAPTER THREE

12 Basic Needs of Every Volunteer 17

    12 Basic Needs 19

    Need 1: A Specific Manageable Task 20

    How to Meet the Need 20

    Need 2: A Task That Matches Motivation 29

    Some Common Volunteer Motives 29

    How to Meet the Need 32

    Need 3: A Good Reason for Doing Task 37

    How to Meet the Need 37

    Need 4: Written Instructions 40

    How to Meet the Need 40

    Need 5: A Reasonable Deadline 44

    How to Meet the Need 44

    Need 6: Freedom to Complete Task 47

    How to Meet the Need 47

    Need 7: Everything Necessary to
Complete Task 50

    How to Meet the Need 50

    Need 8: Adequate Training 53

How to Meet the Need.............................. 53

Need 9: A Safe, Comfortable, Friendly
Environment.. 57

How to Meet the Need............................ 57

Need 10: Follow-up 61

How to Meet the Need............................ 61

Need 11: Opportunity to Provide Feedback........ 68

How to Meet the Need............................ 68

Need 12: Appreciation, Recognition,
and Rewards 72

How to Meet the Need............................ 72

CHAPTER FOUR

Planning for Leadership Succession 77

Stages of Volunteer Development.............. 79

Building a Leadership Cadre 80

Models for Organizing Volunteers............. 83

Reaping Long-Term Benefits of Meeting
Volunteers' Needs 86

CHAPTER FIVE

Case Studies 87

Appendix

Self-Evaluation Checklist....................... 115

ABOUT THE AUTHOR 119

Introduction

Volunteers: How to Get Them, How to Keep Them is dedicated to helping you, the volunteer leaders and staff of nonprofit organizations, solve your volunteer shortages. This book focuses on 12 basic needs of every volunteer and volunteer leader that, if recognized and met, will help you compete for your share of your members' time and talents.

This book grew out of my work with the boards of directors and staffs of a wide variety of professional, trade, educational, charitable, and similar nonprofit membership associations during the past 20 years. Time and time again, both volunteers and association staff voiced concern over the lack of talented and experienced volunteers who are willing to take over the leadership of their organizations. It is not uncommon for this problem to be so severe that independent local organizations and chapters of statewide and national associations become dormant because there is not a single leader to keep the closest-to-home level of the organization going.

There is also considerable concern over the lack of talented and experienced volunteers to carry out the work of the organizations. Volunteers are at the heart of every nonprofit association in the United States. In most nonprofit organizations, projects and events could not be completed without the substantial donation of labor, knowledge, and time by member volunteers. While volunteers are willing to donate their time and talents, it is up to you, the volunteer leaders and staff, to make certain that they choose your association as the recipient of their contributions.

Recruiting, nurturing, and retaining volunteers is typically a cooperative effort between an association's volunteer leaders and its staff. While both groups express concern over the lack of top-level leaders, they frequently fail to recognize that the root of the problem is the lack of experienced volunteers at the closest-to-home level, from which the future leaders for all levels evolve.

While volunteers could ask for what they need when it is not provided, most do not. They merely walk away without telling you why. Recognizing what volunteers need and knowing how to meet those needs will help you increase the number of volunteers and the number of hours each gives to your organization. Seeing that their volunteer experiences are positive will keep your volunteers coming back and also lead to their evolution from volunteers to volunteer leaders, ensuring the continuation of leadership needed for your association to survive and thrive.

This guide provides practical and proven methods for approaching volunteer recruitment and retention. It serves as a permanent, easy-to-use reference for volunteer officers, board members, committee chairs, and staff in all types and sizes of nonprofit membership organizations from the local to the international level.

If you are a volunteer, reading this book may bring back memories of personal experiences in volunteering that were very frustrating because your needs were not understood and met. You can help the volunteer leaders and staff of those organizations by giving them this book as a gift. If you are a volunteer leader or staff member who received this book from one of your members, you are lucky that he or she is concerned enough about your organization to give it to you instead of merely taking his or her contributions elsewhere.

Some terms are used in slightly different ways by various nonprofit organizations, so I have defined the terms as they are used in this book:

A "volunteer" is a person who works in some way to help others for no monetary pay.

"Volunteer leaders" are individuals who serve as officers, board members, and committee chairs, and are responsible for getting and keeping volunteers from within the membership to help carry out the organization's activities.

"Project team leaders" are volunteers or staff, paid or unpaid, who recruit, supervise, and support a team of members who, in turn, oversee work teams of volunteers of their own. In this book the term is used synonymously with volunteer coordinators and volunteer supervisors.

"Members" are individuals who voluntarily join associations and remain on the organization's roster by paying annual dues. In nonprofit organizations that do not have members, the needs of donors and others who perform work without monetary pay are similar to the needs of member volunteers. The suggestions in this book may be modified to apply to these organizations.

"Association" refers to a nonprofit institution or organization incorporated in the USA and recognized as tax-exempt by the IRS. The term is intended to include the variety of terms used by nonprofit organizations — societies, institutes, organizations, alliances, foundations, councils, conferences, boards, and leagues. It includes all types of nonprofit organizations that are dependent upon volunteers to carry on the activities of their organizations.

"Chapter" refers to an independent local organization or the local, closest-to-home level of a district, regional, state, national, or international organization. The term is intended to include the variety of terms used for that level — chapters, local or county societies, guilds, leagues, bureaus, components, and similar terms.

The main text of this book is organized into five main parts. Chapter One discusses the myth and reality of the current volunteer shortage. Chapter Two discusses managing expectations regarding volunteering. Chapter Three presents 12 basic needs of every volunteer and volunteer leader and suggestions for meeting those needs. Chapter Four discusses planning for leadership succession in your organization. Chapter Five contains case studies of real volunteer experiences, analyses of what was done to meet the volunteers' needs, and suggestions for what could have been done to make the experiences better. It provides an opportunity for you to rate two organizations' performances in meeting volunteers' needs. The Appendix contains a self-evaluation checklist to help volunteer leaders and staff assess how well their organizations are meeting volunteers' needs.

CHAPTER ONE

The Volunteer Shortage: Myth or Reality

If you are experiencing a shortage of volunteers in your association you are not alone. Voluntary membership organizations, large and small, are having difficulty getting and keeping talented volunteers to carry on their activities. Board members and staff frequently identify less time donated by volunteers as a trend of critical importance to their associations.

What has caused this shortage? Quite simply, the laws of supply and demand. On the demand side, the number of nonprofit organizations in the USA today is estimated at more than one million. While there is no single source that states the exact number of nonprofits, several credible sources reveal these statistics:

• **The Web site of the Internet Nonprofit Center (http//www.nonprofits.org/loc/) contains a searchable database of more than one million nonprofit associations, not including some religious organizations.** Local units of national groups may be included with the "umbrella" registration of the parent organization, and may not be listed separately.

• **The *Statistical Abstract of the United States* reports 22,901 national nonprofit organizations in the United States.** [1]

• **Additionally, there are thousands of nonprofits in each state — reportedly 120,000 in California alone.** [2]

All of these nonprofits are competing for volunteers' time, talents, and energy. The situation has become more competitive because many organizations have suffered cutbacks in resources that have led to an increase in their need for volunteers.

---

[1] U.S. Bureau of Census, *Statistical Abstract of the United States: 1998,* (118th Edition.) Washington, DC, 1998. Table 1295. p. 777.

[2] *Dateline,* February 1997, Northern California Society of Association Executives, San Francisco, CA, p. 8.

On the supply side, there are many macroenvironmental trends that affect the availability of volunteers. As a whole, people are seeking more balance in their lives, leaving less time for volunteer work. More than a decade of corporate downsizing has resulted in people doing more with fewer resources at work. This has caused more stress in their lives and has left them less willing to give up valuable personal time to volunteer. Additionally, because most American adults must work, they are highly discriminating in their use of time.

Volunteer opportunities that require long-term commitments, such as lengthy terms of office and committee membership, are intimidating to those whose time is already at a premium. Such broad, undefined tasks are barriers to getting members involved for the first time. This leads to a shortage of experienced volunteers ready to replace key officers, board members, and committee chairs, and ultimately results in the burnout of many experienced volunteers who continue to fill one or more of these positions year after year.

While many associations are facing a serious shortage of volunteers, a number of statistics show that, even in today's environment, American adults continue to volunteer.

- According to the 1998 *Statistical Abstract of the United States*, 49% of the adult population did volunteer work in 1995. [3]

- In a 1996 study by Independent Sector, a coalition of 800 corporations, foundations, and nonprofit organizations that studies nonprofit organizations, it was reported that 93 million American adults did volunteer work in 1995, totaling 20.3 billion hours, or 4.2 hours per person per week. The total assigned dollar value of volunteer time was estimated to be $201.5

---

[3] *Statistical Abstract of the United States*, p. 396.

billion.[4] That is greater than the annual gross domestic product of such countries as: Chile, Egypt, Greece, Finland, Norway, Sweden, Denmark, Switzerland, and Venezuela! [5]

Who is volunteering? The *Statistical Abstract* reports the following:

- **Americans between the ages of 25 and 54 are most likely to volunteer.** More than half of the people in this age group reported doing some work for no monetary pay during the previous year.

- **Forty-five percent of all American men and 52% of all American women volunteer.**

- **Volunteering increases with educational attainment, with 70% of college graduates donating an average of 4.8 hours per week.**

- **Volunteering increases with household income, with 69% of those with household incomes of $100,000 or more reporting volunteering.** [6]

Where are these men and women taking their time and talents? According to a variety of studies, people are most likely to volunteer for charitable and community service projects. Very little data is available about what portion of this volunteer time is donated by members to their organizations for other types of volunteer activities — serving as officers, board members, or committee service, and helping to carry on a wide variety of programs and activities.

---

[4] Hodgkinson, Virginia, Murray, Weitzmen, and the Gallop Organization, Inc. *Giving and Volunteering in the United States,* 1996 Edition. Independent Sector. Washington, DC, Fall 1996.

[5] *The World Almanac and Book of Facts 1999,* World Almanac Books, PRIMEDIA Reference, Inc. Mahwah, New Jersey. pp. 760-861.

[6] *Statistical Abstract of the United States,* p. 396.

Many people want to "make a difference" so they join and volunteer in charitable organizations that solve a problem or contribute to a greater good. This is good news if yours is a charitable organization, but it presents a challenge for other types of nonprofit associations. Many trade and professional organizations are finding that it is difficult to compete for their members' volunteer time. The number of members willing to work simply because you need them, or because of a desire to give back to their industry or profession, is rapidly diminishing.

Americans continue to volunteer, but demand for volunteers exceeds the supply. In such an environment, you'll have to work harder and smarter to get your members to choose your organization as the recipient of their time and to keep them coming back. Volunteers keep mental lists of what they give and what they get from the relationship. If you don't meet their needs, they will go to someone who will.

CHAPTER TWO

Setting the Stage

The process of matching a task to a volunteer begins long before the task is actually assigned. It begins the day a new member joins your organization. From the beginning, you need to set the stage so members will expect to help with your organization's activities.

Managing Volunteers' Expectations

People come to a charitable organization because they want to contribute to a cause they support. They expect to give of themselves. On the other hand, people join professional and trade associations to get the benefits of membership. In an eagerness to get people to join, membership recruiters focus on what the organization will do for the prospect. Recruiters tell prospects about how they will benefit from all of the programs, services, and activities provided to members by the association. They often fail to let prospects know that, as a membership organization, there must be meaningful involvement from many members to carry on the programs and activities year to year. Expectations will vary depending on the type of organization. Letting members know what opportunities exist in their chapter soon after they join opens the door to participation, first at the chapter level, and then at other levels of the organization. Advertising for volunteers in newsletters and making announcements at meetings serve as constant reminders to members that their time and talents are the lifeblood of a healthy organization.

While voluntarism is a concept that is widely accepted in North America, it is not universally understood and expected around the world. If you have chapters in other parts of the world, setting the expectation up front that members will be asked to perform a wide variety of tasks without pay is of critical importance to successful volunteer recruitment and retention.

Managing Your Expectations

No matter how valiant your efforts, not everyone will volunteer. Even in the healthiest of membership organizations, experience reveals the percentages in the pyramid below to be realistic (Figure 1).

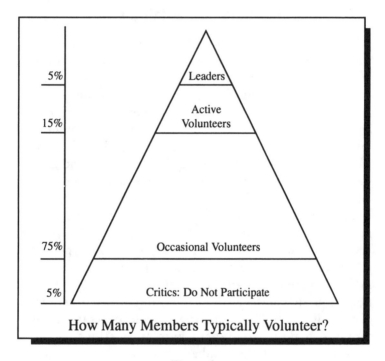

Figure 1

- Approximately 5% of the membership serve as volunteer leaders: officers, board members, and key committee and task force chairs.

- Another 15% of the membership are active volunteers: project team leaders and work team leaders.

- Approximately 75% of the membership volunteer occasionally, participate in some activities, and use some services.

- **The remaining 5% are critics.** You've probably noticed that they do not participate but tend to complain about everything. This group keeps the other 95% from becoming complacent.

- **It is up to you, the most active 20% of the members, to attract and keep volunteers from the 75% who are occasional participants and not let the 5% who are the critics siphon off your energy.**

CHAPTER THREE

12 Basic Needs of Every Volunteer

12 Basic Needs

There are 12 basic needs that all volunteers and volunteer leaders share. These are needs that must be met if volunteers are to be successful and if you are to retain them year after year.

1. A specific manageable task with a beginning and an end.

2. A task that matches interests and reasons for volunteering.

3. A good reason for doing the task.

4. Written instructions.

5. A reasonable deadline for completing the task.

6. Freedom to complete the task *when* and *where* it is most convenient for the volunteer.

7. Everything necessary to complete the task without interruption.

8. Adequate training.

9. A safe, comfortable, and friendly working environment.

10. Follow-up to see that the task is completed.

11. An opportunity to provide feedback when the task is finished.

12. Appreciation, recognition, and rewards that match the reasons for volunteering.

Recognizing these needs and knowing how to meet them will help you expand the number of members who volunteer and increase the number of hours each gives to your association. The remainder of this book is dedicated to helping you recognize and meet these needs.

> *1. A volunteer needs a specific manageable task with a beginning and an end.*

The Need

A feeling of success is needed to sustain volunteers' efforts. Broad and vague goals can be frustrating to volunteers because they don't know what they are being asked to do and therefore don't know when they will be finished with their commitment. This leads to wasted resources and rapid turnover. This can be avoided by organizing volunteers into work groups, each working on one or more specific tasks that are achievable. When combined with other tasks, progress is made toward a larger achievable goal. Volunteers, especially new volunteers, need to know exactly what they are being asked to do and how much time it will take.

How to Meet the Need

Take Time to Plan and Get Organized.

Often volunteers are asked to work on a project before project team leaders are recruited, the tasks are defined, and the preparation is complete. As a result, time and talents are wasted and volunteers lose interest. It is up to you, the volunteer leaders and staff, to recruit a project team leader for each major program or activity. Before asking members to volunteer, each project team leader must take time to think the project through and do adequate pre-planning.

• **Determine the deadline for completing the project.** For major projects set interim deadlines. If you are planning an annual conference, deadlines for selecting the site, completing the program topics, contracting speakers, and mailing the registration materials are examples of important interim deadlines to establish up front.

- **Break the project down into groups of major tasks to be done.** If your project is large or complex, recruit a project team of experienced volunteers, each to be responsible for a group of major tasks. For example, if you are responsible for planning the programs at 10 monthly meetings, you could recruit five team members to plan two meetings each. Or, you could recruit five teams members and make one responsible for publicity for all meetings, another for logistics, another for speakers, and another for registration. These project team members would then create work groups as needed to help complete their part of the project.

- **If your project is smaller, break the project down into small tasks that are achievable in a short time and will not intimidate new volunteers.** For a one-day telephone fund-raising campaign, smaller, manageable tasks may include preparing call lists, securing a site, planning food and hospitality, recruiting volunteer callers, preparing and conducting training, and tracking and reporting progress.

- **Clearly define each task to help ensure that a member will agree to volunteer and that the task will be completed.** Include all required parameters for how the task is to be completed. If you recruit volunteers to "welcome new members," they may interpret that as greeting them personally when, in fact, you intend for them to call new members. If you recruit volunteers to work at a telephone bank but provide no details, they are likely to say no. You will probably get better results if you ask a volunteer to join a group of 10 other volunteers at your office to make welcoming calls to new members for two hours.

- Using the list of tasks, estimate how much time each will require. Develop a timeline.

- Determine how many volunteers you will need. Keep in mind that the more volunteers you recruit the less work each has to do.

- Determine the level of experience that a given volunteer needs to complete each task. This depends on the amount of risk involved if the task is not completed or is done poorly; for example, a task with the potential for high risk of financial loss, legal exposure, or negative publicity should be given to an experienced volunteer.

- Determine what information skills and tools the volunteer must already have and which of these items you will provide.

- Design a worksheet for each project. The more complex the project the more detailed your planning worksheet will be. See the sample Project Planning Worksheet in Example 1 on the following page.

Don't Wait for Members to Volunteer — Recruit the Best Person for the Job.

A volunteer is a person who works in some way to help others without pay. The term suggests that a person must offer herself or himself to perform a service without being asked to do so. However, volunteers can be recruited — you don't have to wait for people to offer. *Ask them!*

- Avoid limiting your list of potential volunteers to your friends and current volunteers. Collect all sources of potential volunteers — results of interest surveys, project reports, volunteer database, staff and board recommendations. Creating a diverse volunteer group that is representative of all segments of your membership is the first step in creating a diverse group of volunteer leaders and officers.

Project Planning Worksheet *

Description of task/task group (one per sheet): *Secure speaker for September15th chapter meeting with signed contract*

Estimated time required: *1-2 hours*

Risk level (high, limited, none): *Limited*

Deadline(s) for reporting progress: *15th of each month from April until contract is signed.*

Deadline for completing task: *July 15*

Deadline for final reporting and evaluation: *September 30*

Information, skills, tools needed for task	Volunteer already has	I need to provide
Project goals/objectives	X	
Budget for speaker fee and travel		X
Meeting times/dates		X
Guidelines/parameters for task		X
Reimbursement policy	X	
List of potential speakers		X
Speaker contract		X

Five volunteers with skills and experience to match task:
1. ~~*Marian White*~~   2. ~~*Jim Green*~~   3. *Susan Samuels*
4. *Rachael Harrow* 5. *Xavier Hernandez*

Assigned to: *Susan Samuels* (Marian and Jim declined.)

Status (dates, notes of all contact, reports, problems to address): *Confirmed in writing to Susan January 30th.*

Example 1

* Information for downloading a master copy of this form from the Internet is located on the last page of this book.

Consider age, gender, race, membership categories, job, and company size and type as you build your volunteer teams.

- Recruit experienced volunteers to be project team leaders to oversee and coordinate teams of newer and less-involved volunteers.

- Fill high-risk tasks that require experienced and proven volunteers first.

- Some experienced volunteers will probably want to continue to do specific tasks and not want to take on more responsibility or donate more time. If this is the case, don't scare them away by applying too much pressure to take on more responsibility. Let them continue to contribute by assigning them tasks with which they are familiar. If you meet their needs, they are more likely to continue to be involved and some may eventually agree to give you more time and accept more responsibility.

- Contact new prospects. Assign low-risk tasks to new volunteers until they prove to be dependable.

- Even if a member says no when asked, the fact that you asked makes that member aware of the need for volunteers. It lets that member know that there is a place for him or her to volunteer in the future.

- Don't ask everyone. Narrow the field. Make a list of names and telephone numbers of five people you think would be good for the task in order of who would be the best fit with the job, who would be the second best, and so on.

- Ask the best prospect first instead of asking the person who is most likely to say yes. Asking the best person for the job lets that person know that it is important that he or she gets personally involved. Members will likely feel flattered to be asked.

- **Recruit one-to-one in person, on the phone, or in written communication.** Ask a specific person to do a specific task. The more specific the request, the more likely the person is to say yes.

- **Assume people will say yes.** People like to be asked. It shows that you respect their work.

- **If members are not available when you need them, or are not interested in doing the task you suggested, perhaps they will agree to another task or time.** Whenever possible have more than one task from which the member can choose. Be flexible and willing to adjust your request to meet the member's needs.

- **It is best if the person who will be working directly with the volunteer does the asking.** If you do not personally know anyone in the group of people from whom you are recruiting, ask other volunteer leaders and staff who are closer to them for their input on your list of prospects.

Personalize Your Request.

- **Assess members' interests and preferences for volunteer activities when you contact them with a volunteer opportunity.**

- **Be specific.** Ask them "Will you help me with . . .?" or "Can I count on you to help me with . . .?" Don't wait for them to offer.

- **Use published notices of volunteer opportunities in your newsletters to remind members that their time and talents are essential elements in the organization.** However, actually recruit volunteers one-to-one at meetings, via telephone, or in writing.

- **If you must recruit volunteers from outside your membership, publishing notices in newspapers and corporate and community newsletters creates an awareness of your need and gives you visibility.** Follow up by contacting businesses and organized groups whose employees or members support your mission. Propose a mutually beneficial project.

- **Don't stand up at a meeting and ask members who are interested in helping to contact you or sign up on a sheet that is being circulated around the room.** This communicates that "anyone" can do the job at hand when actually you want the best person for the job. Furthermore, individual members can slip out of the room, feeling that someone else will surely respond. Instead, announce that you are seeking volunteers and that you will be coming around the room (or calling) to ask for help. See Example 2 below.

☹ *These practices, although common, are not likely to produce the best results:*

"The awards committee needs more members. If anyone is interested in joining our committee, please see me after the meeting."

"Anyone who wants to be on the awards committee, sign your name on the sheet that is being circulated around the room before you leave tonight"

☺ *You'll get better results with the following:*

"I volunteered to coordinate the annual awards program. There are many tasks to be done, some that take only a couple of hours, like working registration, and some that you can do at home or in your office, like judging one category of entries. I'll be coming around the room tonight and calling this week to ask some of you for help."

Example 2

Ask Members to Commit to Short Blocks of Time.

- **Start by asking a member who has never volunteered for a two-hour time block.** For example, ask him or her to work at the registration table for a two-hour shift. Even when members commit to completing a small task, they are concerned about not being able to get away when they finish. Many worry that they will be expected to become as active as their leaders if they commit to the smallest task. Designating an ending time assures them that this fear is unfounded.

- **When volunteers complete the time block they committed to, thank them and let them go.** If you need more time or you want them for another task, negotiate with them. Leave the door open to come back to them at a later date.

- **Recruit new volunteers for task forces and ad hoc assignments.** Task forces have clear assignments, and when the work is completed the task force is disbanded. This is distinctly different from committees, which are ongoing and frequently have no specific task assigned. New committee members show up in the beginning but lose interest when meetings drag on or are poorly attended. Asking a member to serve on a membership task force created to determine the rights, benefits, and dues level for a new category of membership would produce better results then asking him or her to serve on the membership committee.

- **Limit meetings to meaningful activities such as planning, coordinating activities, making adjustments, making decisions, and performing tasks that require collective wisdom.** Don't waste valuable volunteer time disseminating information that could have been mailed or e-mailed. Require only individuals who need to be present to attend. Committees are notorious for holding meetings that members consider a waste of time.

If time spent in meetings is not meaningful, volunteers will stop attending.

- As a volunteer gets more involved, ask for commitments for longer blocks of time and assign more complex projects. Ask him or her to coordinate a work team of newer volunteers.

- In some cases the member does not want to become more involved. See if he or she will volunteer for a task that requires a regular schedule but requires only a short block of time each week or month and involves no additional responsibilities.

In addition to having many positive benefits for the volunteers, recruiting volunteers for finite periods also provides valuable benefits for you. It opens the door for many members to be involved in some way. It allows you to assess their talents and skills, and identify those who can be relied on to complete high-risk tasks. It also prevents a volunteer from serving in a capacity too long when he or she is not performing, or when there is a need for "new blood" in the organization.

> 2. A volunteer needs a task that matches interests and reasons for volunteering.

The Need

Each volunteer has his or her own reasons for volunteering in your organization. What motivates one might not motivate another. Some volunteer leaders make the mistake of assuming that all members volunteer for the same reasons they do; for example, a shared purpose, personal recognition, or to contribute to a good cause. When recruiting and managing volunteers, it is important to recognize these differences and match the tasks, work environment, and rewards to the individual's own reasons for volunteering. For instance, a member may want to serve on a board or a visible committee because of the prestige and associated credentials, but may not want to do any work. It is your responsibility to clearly define the role of a board member and the work that is involved, and to find potential candidates who have matching motives.

Some Common Volunteer Motives

Affiliation/Socialization

Some people who work or live alone want to break the isolation by working with others. Some like to be with other people to make contacts and new friends, or to expand their circle of acquaintances through volunteer activities. Give them tasks that require personal interaction and assign group projects. Build time for socializing into each agenda, but don't let socializing replace work in these groups.

Challenge

These people need specific goals. They stick to the task and work well alone. Give them measurable goals and tasks that have closure, such as membership campaigns or fundraising drives. Some people like handling difficult work. Try to match them up with activities that intellectually stimulate them. Start with smaller pieces of a bigger project before turning over total responsibility to them for your organization's more complex initiatives.

Creativity/Self-Expression

These people like to contribute new ideas with originality and inventiveness. Give them tasks where they can use their natural talent, ability, and creativity, with sufficient direction to ensure that the creativity is channeled to achieve project goals. These people like to plan the entertainment for a group and develop promotional campaigns.

Independence

These people prefer to work on their own, free from supervision. Let them work in their homes or offices on their own schedule. Be sure to give them clear directions and parameters up front so that the end product and time frame meet your objectives.

Leadership/Power/Prestige

These people seek highly visible positions of authority and prestige and respond well to titles. Once they have proved to be dependable, give them tasks that require them to plan, organize, and direct others. If these people are already well known, their involvement may add credibility to a fund-raising project or event merely because their names are associated with it.

Recognition

While all members need recognition for their work, these members volunteer primarily to get public recognition for their contribution. Like those who seek positions of authority or prestige, these people are interested in high-profile positions such as officers, leaders, and key committees. Some seek positions that allow them to work with high-profile or important people.

Security

These are the people who like familiar and comfortable tasks. Let them stick with tasks they like. They are good candidates for tasks that must be performed on a regular schedule year after year.

Self-Improvement

Self-improvement is a common reason that members volunteer in professional and trade associations today. These people desire self-advancement and growth. They want to gain new skills in a safe environment, or maintain or sharpen current skills. Match them up with experienced volunteers who possess the skills they desire, or train them to perform the tasks you lay out for them. They make good understudies for newsletter editors, treasurers, and major event chairpersons.

Sense of Duty

The number of members who volunteer because they think they should or because they want to give back to their organization or profession is decreasing in today's environment. These members have probably been volunteers for many years. They sometimes tend to suffer from the "If I don't do it, it won't get done" martyr complex. They are not the best volunteers, but will help out when you need them.

Service/Interest in Cause

These people want to help others and work on cause-oriented tasks. Use them for community service projects, to promote the industry or profession, or let them work on awards and scholarships. A person known for his or her support of the arts may make the ideal chairperson of the annual fund-raising drive to benefit the local art museum.

Variety

These members seek diverse activities. They like a change of scene and tasks. They get bored easily and like to change assignments when they have mastered a task. They are often good troubleshooters and can fill in where you need them. Look to them when you need to fill a vacancy.

How to Meet the Need

- **Try to match tasks to members' interests and motives as noted in the examples above.**

- **Give members choices.** A member may dislike telephone work but be willing to be a greeter at meetings.

- **Don't assume you know what volunteers prefer — ask them.** If a volunteer has small children, he or she may want to get out of the house for adult company. The member who uses the computer regularly at work may not want to spend any more time at the computer and may prefer tasks that are outdoors or that involve a great deal of activity.

- **Make sure that members' interests match the skills needed for a project.** If a member wants to learn meeting planning skills, pair him or her up with an experienced volunteer leader who is planning an educational conference. Don't count on an inexperienced person to plan the conference without first gaining the needed skills.

- At the chapter level, survey the interests and preferences of members both when they join and on a regular basis thereafter.

- If yours is a state-level organization, survey the pool of experienced volunteer leaders from your chapters to assess their interests in becoming volunteers at the state level.

- If yours is a national-level organization, survey the state leaders, and so on. Modify the following sample cover letter and preference survey in Examples 3 and 4 to fit your situation.

To: Karen Marino
From: Jacob Bernstein, XYZ Chapter President
Re: Preferences for volunteer activities

Our chapter is able to carry on our activities because of the generosity of you and other member volunteers. There are many tasks that need to be done throughout the year. Some take only a few hours and some require a one-year commitment. Some can even be done in your home or office. I am writing to ask you to consider volunteering for one or more of these tasks during the coming year.

Please review the enclosed list of skills and resources we need and check all of those that appeal to you. We will try to match your interests with a specific activity. A volunteer leader will be calling you soon to discuss your preferences. I hope you will commit to giving us your time and talents again this year.

A warm thank you,

Jacob

Example 3

Member Name: Karen Marino
Member ID: 50500

Preferences for Volunteer Activities *

I've checked each of the skills and resources I may be willing to make available to the chapter at least once during the coming year:

☐   Being a table host at a monthly meeting.

☐   Conducting marketing research.

☐   Contributing to a community service project.

☐   Desktop publishing, graphic design.

☐   Donating printing of materials (brochures, newsletters, posters).

☐   Editing articles for newsletters.

☐   Helping with newsletter mailings.

☐   Hosting prospective members at breakfasts.

☐   Introducing a speaker.

☐   Leading a roundtable discussion.

☐   Maintaining membership database, printing labels, mailing renewals.

☐   Making meeting arrangements for monthly meetings.

☐   Moderating a panel discussion.

☐   Monitoring governmental or regulatory activities in my home district.

☐   Serving as a panel member for panel discussion.

☐   Telephoning prospective members to invite them to meetings.

☐   Telephoning prospects after they have attended a meeting.

☐   Use of my business for a chapter meeting.

☐   Use of my home for a chapter meeting.

☐   Working registration at one monthly meeting.

☐   Writing articles for newsletters.

☐   Speaking at a meeting on the following topic(s):_____

_____

☐   Conducting a workshop on the follow topic(s):_____

_____

☐   Other:_____

_____

Example 4

I'm interested in becoming more involved in the following areas (check all that apply):

☐ Campaigns

☐ Community service projects

☐ Computer, database, Web site, and technology projects

☐ Corporate sponsorships/fund raising

☐ Financial planning, budgeting, accounting, audits

☐ Government relations/regulatory

☐ Group buying discounts/insurance

☐ Marketing/PR/sales

☐ Meeting and event planning

☐ Membership

☐ Newsletter

Best day(s) of week for volunteer work (check all that apply):

☐ Monday

☐ Tuesday

☐ Wednesday

☐ Thursday

☐ Friday

☐ Saturday

☐ Sunday

Best time of day for volunteer work (check all that apply):

☐ Before 8:00 a.m.

☐ 8:00 to 10:00 a.m.

☐ 10:00 to 12:00 noon

☐ 12:00 to 2:00 p.m.

☐ 2:00 to 4:00 p.m.

☐ 4:00 to 6:00 p.m.

☐ 6:00 to 8:00 p.m.

☐ 8:00 to 10:00 p.m.

I've served as a leader in these nonprofit organizations in recent years:

_____

_____

Please return in the envelope provided. Thank you.

Example 4 continued

*Information for downloading a master copy of this form from the Internet is located on the last page of this book.

- Create a system to keep track of volunteers' interests, projects assigned, successes, and problems. Keep the system simple. The widespread use of personal computers makes it possible for virtually every size association to develop such a system using a database program such as Microsoft Access. Ensure that project team leaders keep current records of volunteer service. Some associations assign the task of tracking volunteers' interests and service to one volunteer.

- It is *extremely* important to follow through and contact members who have indicated an interest in volunteering and recruit them to work in one of their areas of interest. If you get more volunteers than you can use for a specific activity, contact those volunteers whom you will not need to make them aware of the situation. Ask if they will agree to do other tasks. Use them to fill vacancies that occur during the year.

- If a member is not interested in the task you offer, offer alternatives. Listen and make notes when the member talks about his or her interests. If another project interests him or her, pass the name along to the appropriate project team leader.

Keep in mind that members volunteer for their own personal reasons, not yours. Taking the time to find out what motivates and interests them, and matching those individual preferences with the tasks to be done, will pay off in the quality and quantity of work completed.

---

3. A volunteer needs a good reason for doing the task.

The Need

If work is not meaningful, do not ask volunteers to do it. Volunteers need to know that their contribution is important. They find time to work on projects that contribute to goals that they support. They are motivated when they gain in some way — a new skill, new relationships, a feeling that what they did made a difference. Volunteers are more likely to complete tasks and do so on time when they know that others are counting on them.

How to Meet the Need

- **If the work is not important, stop doing it.** If a task or project is not a critical element of your overall mission, goals, or strategic plan, why is it being done? Review all standing committees and eliminate those that are filled year after year, but have nothing to do, and those for which no one wants to volunteer.

- **Tell the volunteers that what they are doing is important to the organization.** Help them understand the importance of their contribution — how each task fits into a bigger project or objective. Tell them what's at stake if the work is not done well and on time. Remind them of what's in it for them, based on their reasons for volunteering.

- **Let them know you have selected them as the best person for the job and that they aren't merely the first person who said yes.**

- **Develop an action plan early in the project.** Include the overall project goals and objectives, steps that will be taken, the person responsible for each action, and the deadline for completion.
- **Create a project activity tracking form for each project.** Use the table function in Microsoft Word or a spreadsheet in Microsoft Excel or similar programs that will allow you to sort by columns. Include all activities from your action plan as described above. Add dates of meetings, conference calls, and dates status reports are due. Sort the columns by "Who," "Deadline," or "Status" to monitor the plan as time progresses. Distribute a copy to each volunteer up front and just prior to each reporting date to remind team members of deadlines and to create peer pressure to get the tasks completed. This lets them know that others are counting on them. See the sample Project Activity Tracking Form in Example 5 on the next page.

By communicating the importance of the task to volunteers, and by letting them know that others are counting on their contribution, they will feel a greater sense of importance and thus give a greater level of commitment to the task.

Project Activity Tracking Form *

Project description: Call members who haven't renewed by September 1[st.]

Project team leader: James

Project team members: Howard, Sam, Muriel, Sharon

Action item	Who	Deadline	Status
Schedule office for phone bank 7-9 p.m.	James	Aug. 1	
Recruit six volunteers to make calls on Oct. 1	Muriel	Sep. 1	
Confirm details in writing to each volunteer	Muriel	Sep. 1	
Create and mail meeting notice	James	Sep. 15	
Print out call lists	Sam	Sep. 30	
Write calling instructions	Howard	Oct. 1	
Plan and bring snacks	Sharon	Oct. 1	
Conduct training for callers	Howard	Oct. 1	
File report with office	James	Oct. 2	
Send thank you notes to volunteers	Sharon	Oct. 15	

Example 5

*Information for downloading a master copy of this form from the Internet is located on the last page of this book.

1. A volunteer needs written instructions.

The Need

A volunteer needs a clear understanding of the commitment and expectations to ensure success. Communicating the specifics in writing will increase the odds that he or she will say yes and that the task will be completed satisfactorily.

The lack of a clear contract between a volunteer and the project team leader presents a basic problem. In the eagerness to get volunteers to commit, details regarding the expectations may not be communicated clearly. There may be a misunderstanding about exactly what the volunteer has agreed to do. If nothing is confirmed in writing, members may verbally commit to complete a task but then forget the details, or forget the commitment altogether.

How to Meet the Need

Follow up all verbal commitments with a written thank you and details of the agreement. It is important to use your organization's letterhead for this and all other communication to volunteers. See sample letter in Example 6 on the following page.

(letterhead)

Dear Maurie,

Thank you for volunteering to introduce the speaker at the June luncheon of ABC Riverside. Here are the details of our telephone conversation on Monday:

The luncheon will be held on Friday, June 21, in the ballroom at the Harborside Inn in Riverside. The inn is located at 32234 Marina Drive. A map and directions to the inn are enclosed along with parking information. *

Please call Joan at 702-555-9922 to register in advance to ensure that your name badge and meal ticket will be waiting for you. I have to ask you to pay for your lunch because I have no budget for team members' expenses.

I will meet you at the registration desk outside of the ballroom at 11:30 a.m. The speaker is Jane Smart. I've enclosed a brief biography and a description of her presentation. The introduction can be up to four minutes long. When Jane arrives, please act as her host for the meeting. Escort her to your reserved table in the center of the room in front of the podium. Feel free to invite six other members to join your table for lunch.

President Maria James will introduce you after lunch. Proceed to the podium and make your introduction.

After Jane finishes her presentation, go back to the podium, thank her, and present her with the gift that you will find on a shelf inside the podium.

Thank you for agreeing to help me. I am looking forward to working with you. If you need anything else or have questions, please contact me at 888-555-3465 or mary@fastmail.com.

Sincerely,

Mary

Mary Esterbury
Project Team Leader, Monthly Meetings
ABC Riverside

Enclosures (*Be certain that you include all materials that you say you are enclosing.)

Example 6

- Provide clearly written instructions for *what* you want. Tell volunteers what the budget is, the time and dates of any meetings you expect them to attend, interim deadlines, reporting dates, and any other details. Tell the volunteers when and how any missing information, training, and tools will be provided, and by whom.

- As volunteers mature and prove themselves, give them as much freedom as possible to decide *how* the task will be completed. If you have specific expectations or parameters related to *how* the task is to be done, tell them up front.

- Give volunteers the opportunity to ask questions and ask for what they need.

- Complete a Volunteer Task Assignment Worksheet and give a copy to the volunteer. Retain a copy for your project notebook. See a sample Volunteer Task Assignment Worksheet in Example 7 on the following page.

Volunteer Task Assignment Worksheet		
Date: *March 22*		
Volunteer name/contact information: *Susan Samuels* *Tel: 888-555-6789 E-mail: ssamuels@air.com*		
Project team leader's name/contact information: *John Jones* *Tel: 888-555-2344 E-mail: jjones@coolmail.com*		
Description of task: *Secure speaker for September15th chapter meeting. Secure contract and forward it to me for signatures. Obtain speaker bio and forward it to me.*		
Estimated time required: *1-2 hours*		
Deadline(s) for reporting: *15th of each month beginning in April until speaker contract is signed and forwarded to me*		
Deadline for completing: *July 15th*		
Deadline for summary report/evaluation: *September 30th*		
	See attached	Will be provided *
Information needed:		
Project goals/objectives	X	
Speaker honorarium	X	
Expense guidelines for toll calls and speaker expenses	X	
Suggested topics	X	
Skills needed:		
None		
Tools needed:		
List of known speakers on topic with contact information	X	
Speaker contract	X	
* Tell volunteer when and where items checked in this column will be provided.		

Example 7

> 5 *A volunteer needs a reasonable deadline for completing the task.*

The Need

The best volunteers are typically extremely busy people. Whether an employee or a volunteer, people with conflicting demands prioritize work based on deadlines. Therefore, it is critical that you set a specific due date when assigning a task to a volunteer. Assigning a deadline also signals that the task will end.

How to Meet the Need

- **Set the deadline for completion and tell volunteers about it before they commit to the task.** Confirm the deadline in writing when you confirm the commitment.

- **Plan for interim reports from volunteers performing larger tasks.**

- **Monitor the progress of new volunteers through regular reporting.**

- **Urge volunteers to contact you as early as possible when they cannot meet a deadline.** Perhaps extra resources or a new deadline are needed.

- **Contact volunteers a few days ahead of the due date to remind them of the deadline.** Sending a copy of the Project Activity Tracking Form will serve as a gentle reminder that you are counting on them. See the tracking form that a project team leader sent to an experienced volunteer, Howard, in Example 8 on the following page.

Project Activity Tracking Form			
Project description: Call members who haven't renewed by September 1ˢᵗ and ask them to renew			
Project team leader: James			
Project team members: **Howard**, Sam, Muriel, Sharon			
Action item	Who	Deadline	Status
Schedule office for phone bank 7-9 p.m.	James	Aug. 1	Done
Recruit six volunteers to make calls on Oct. 1	Muriel	Sep. 1	Done
Confirm details in writing to each volunteer	Muriel	Sep. 1	Done
Create and mail meeting notice	James	Sep. 15	
Print out call lists	Sam	Sep. 30	
Write calling instructions	**Howard**	**Oct. 1**	
Plan and bring snacks	Sharon	Oct. 1	
Conduct training for callers	**Howard**	**Oct. 1**	
File report with office	James	Oct. 2	
Send thank you notes to volunteers	Sharon	Oct 15	

Example 8

- **When you check in with the volunteers, make certain they have everything they need to complete the task on time.** If there are obstacles, try to overcome them immediately rather than missing a deadline. See the sample script for telephone call to monitor progress in Example 9 on the following page.

Script for phone call to check progress:
"Hello, Howard. This is James. I am checking in to see how your work on the instructions and training for our callers for our telephone bank is going. (Pause for response.) You should have received a packet containing samples of training programs from me last week. Is there anything else you need from me? (Pause for response to make sure he received the packet.) "Our telephone bank is next Friday, October 1st. Will you be ready by that date? (If not, identify obstacles and try to address them.) Thank you very much for your part of this project. I'll see you next week at the office."

Example 9

Clearly communicating the interim reporting dates and final deadlines when the volunteer initially commits to the task will increase the odds that he or she will complete the task on time.

6. *A volunteer needs the freedom to complete the task when and where it is most convenient for the volunteer.*

The Need

Not all tasks have to be done in meetings. Requiring volunteers to drive to a central location may waste time and exclude some volunteers. Members who work evening and night shifts, travel extensively, or have family responsibilities or lengthy commutes will need more flexibility in *when* and *where* they perform tasks or you will lose them. Volunteers who have already demonstrated they can be counted on to deliver high-quality work on time need the freedom to complete tasks in their homes or offices, or while they travel. Meet these needs and you will increase the odds that they will continue to volunteer for you.

How to Meet the Need

• **To the extent possible, allow volunteers to determine a time and place that's best for them to work.** This communicates that you are sensitive to their need to balance work, personal, family, and volunteer responsibilities.

• **Give volunteers who do not value the networking and social contact provided by group projects the option of working on their own.** Allowing members to complete tasks in their homes and offices increases the chance that they will also provide some additional resources such as clerical support, copying, phone tolls, and postage without cost to your organization.

- Don't assume that a volunteer wants to work alone or in a group. Ask which he or she prefers to make sure.

- Minimize the time and cost of travel by holding meetings only when absolutely necessary. Coordinate efforts via periodic telephone or e-mail communication. With current technologies, state, national, and international organizations frequently hold an initial face-to-face meeting of each project team or committee so members can meet one another, get organized, and divide responsibilities. The remainder of the work is coordinated via telephone, teleconferencing, and e-mail.

- Use available communication technologies for conferencing instead of meetings. It is becoming common for groups to complete their work without ever meeting face-to-face, especially in national and international associations. One such national association distributed a photograph of each group member along with the roster so members felt they knew one another. On-line discussions allow volunteers to communicate with other team members and the project team leader whenever and wherever it is convenient for them. Conference calls provide a forum for group decision making and problem solving, and save both travel time and expense. Emerging technologies are making videoconferencing from the computer a viable alternative to meetings.

- Limit conference calls to one hour. Distribute an agenda and guidelines for participating in advance of the call.

- Train all project team leaders and volunteer leaders to plan and conduct conference calls.

- Monitor volunteers working independently, but don't hover. Again, check progress prior to reporting deadlines to make certain work will be completed on time.

- The more difficult the task, the greater the need to supervise work in groups rather than allowing individuals to work independently.

Allowing volunteers to work independently takes more up-front coordination on your part, but the payoff can far outweigh the extra effort.

> 7. A volunteer needs everything necessary to complete the task without interruption.

The Need

Give volunteers *everything* they need to complete the task without interruption. If a critical element of information, a single tool, or clear instructions are missing, volunteers will probably set the project aside, thus increasing the chances that deadlines will not be met.

How to Meet the Need

- **Think the project through before turning it over to the volunteer.** This helps you determine everything that is needed to complete each task. Completing a Project Planning Worksheet as shown in Example 1 on page 23 for each project will help you identify what is needed.

- **Provide everything they need up front.** Don't expect a volunteer to take the initiative and secure what is needed for the project, especially inexperienced and untested volunteers.

- **If you are counting on a volunteer to provide anything for the project, discuss this when you assign the task.**

- **As volunteers mature and take on more complex tasks, ask them to provide the items needed, but discuss this early to ensure that they can actually provide them.** One statewide organization found that members were willing to pay for teleconference calls, resulting in considerable savings to the association.

- Provide everything that is needed for group work so that when volunteers arrive, their time is not wasted. A list of materials needed to complete four common projects follows:

  1. **Preparing a mailing to members:**
     - Cover letter with a list of packet contents.
     - Instructions for preparing the mailing, with deadlines for mailing and reporting.
     - All materials to be mailed, envelopes, address labels, and stamps.
     - A reporting form.

  2. **Making telephone calls to members who have not renewed:**
     - Cover letter with a list of packet contents.
     - Instructions for making the calls and filling in reports.
     - Script or suggested points to make during the call.
     - Names to call with telephone numbers.
     - A call sheet to record calls.
     - Reporting form and information on when and where to send report.
     - Who to call for help.
     - Suggestions for how to handle common problems.
     - Answers to frequently asked questions.

  3. **Preparing a mailing to members asking them to contact elected officials on an issue:**
     - Cover letter with a list of packet contents.
     - A specific call to action.
     - Names and contact information for their own elected officials.

- A model letter or postcard that can be personalized.

- Clear, step-by-step instructions and a deadline.

- A stamp or stamped envelope, or ask them to provide these items.

- Who to call for help.

4. **Giving a presentation on career day:**

- Cover letter with a list of packet contents.

- Script or talking points.

- Video/computer presentation.

- Lesson plan.

- Multiple copies of handouts.

- Presentation guidelines.

- List of frequently asked questions with suggested answers.

- Who to call for help.

Providing volunteers with everything they need to complete the task will dramatically increase the probability that the task will be completed on time and to your satisfaction.

8. A volunteer needs adequate training.

The Need

Don't assume that volunteers know how to perform a task. Few volunteers will ask for training. Volunteers need training, as do the volunteer leaders who recruit and manage work groups. Each needs to know how to recruit, manage, and retain his or her own team of volunteers.

How to Meet the Need

- Balance your need to get the work done with the volunteer's desire to learn new skills.

- If you've selected the best volunteer for the job, hopefully he or she will have some experience in the job area. Some individuals volunteer to gain new experience. Be patient and reward them with some new skills or experience by training them.

- Match volunteers who have needed skills they are willing to share with volunteers who desire to achieve those same skills.

- Offer alternatives for training. Depending on the complexity of the project and the skills and experience of the volunteers, a short meeting to review a process may be all that is needed for group projects. Holding one-on-one training may be better for training volunteers who are updating membership records in the database. Some people work well if given a brief list of step-by-step instructions for a project, such as a mailing. Use role-playing and scripts to prepare volunteers to make recruitment and fund-raising calls.

- Monitor volunteers following the training to be certain each has acquired the skills needed to complete the task. Offer supplemental training to individuals who do not demonstrate the needed skills.

Thorough planning will help you anticipate the need for training so it can be offered at the onset of the project. This prevents problems that could result in delays and missed deadlines.

Provide Training for Volunteer Leaders

- If you are using volunteers to provide training, train the trainers to make certain they are qualified and prepared to train adults. Provide a written copy of any rules or procedures that you expect volunteer trainers to pass along. Follow up to make sure they are conducting the training properly. Provide regular refresher courses for trainers.

- Conduct chapter leadership training annually.

- District, regional, state, national, and international levels will benefit by investing in training of volunteer leaders in their chapters and other levels of their organization. Today's chapter leaders are tomorrow's state volunteers and leaders — then regional, then national and international. Invest in an annual leadership conference that is loaded with training. Offer incentives such as partial reimbursement of fees to get volunteer leaders from the chapters to attend.

- There are a variety of effective training tools and topics for training volunteer leaders, as follows:

  1. Training tools:

     - Annual leadership conferences.

     - Leadership manuals and handbooks.

- Sample agendas, with times assigned to each agenda item.
- Regular leadership newsletters (may be sent electronically).
- On-line discussion groups.
- Train-the-trainer workshops.
- Packaged presentations and training materials.
- A personal copy of this book, *Volunteers: How to Get Them, How to Keep Them.*

2. **Topics for leadership conferences:**
   - A review of the mission, purpose, and objectives of the association.
   - How to plan meetings.
   - How to create effective meeting notices.
   - How to run a meeting.
   - How to create minutes and action lists.
   - Handling meeting logistics.
   - Conducting meetings on-line.
   - Using teleconferencing for meetings.
   - How to get reports on time.
   - How to recruit volunteers.
   - How to train volunteers, especially adult volunteers.
   - Identifying and meeting volunteers' needs.
   - How to monitor without hovering.
   - Managing volunteers who don't perform.
   - Presentation skills.

- Incorporating networking and fun into activities,

Providing adequate training for volunteers and volunteer leaders is an essential ingredient of volunteer retention and development. By allocating resources to training, your assocation will reap benefits well into the future.

> *9. A volunteer needs a safe, comfortable, and friendly working environment.*

The Need

The safety and welfare of volunteers must be a high priority, especially in urban areas. Insufficient parking, expensive parking fees, and poorly lighted parking lots or entrances may deter volunteers from returning a second time.

In addition to volunteers' safety, it is important to make the volunteering experience as pleasant as possible. A friendly inviting atmosphere helps ensure that the volunteer will leave with the memory of a positive experience. Young volunteers in particular report being turned off by the organizations' failure to address issues related to the working environment.

How to Meet the Need

- **Send a meeting notice containing the address and telephone number of the meeting place.** Include a map, clearly written driving directions, and information about public transportation and parking. Make it easy for the volunteer to attend by removing all possible obstacles.

- **Provide plenty of parking that is affordable or free.** Ensure that parking is easily and safely accessible.

- **Make certain the exterior of your meeting place is well lighted.**

- **Ensure that your meeting place is secure.**

- Arrange for the heat or air conditioning to remain on during evening hours and weekends.

- Provide a clean, uncluttered work area with comfortable chairs.

- Ensure a smoke-free working environment.

- **If volunteers are new, pick them up.** Call to confirm their attendance or pair them up with seasoned volunteers.

- **Meet people at the door.** Quickly introduce them to another member of the group so you can move on to other attendees. Allow time for volunteers to get acquainted.

- **Show people around.** Do anything else you can to make them feel comfortable and welcome.

- **Have nametags with first names ready for everyone in the group, including yourself.** Hand write them clearly in large letters or print them in a point size of at least 36 to make certain that names are readable across a table. Don't clutter nametags with too much information.

- **If it is important for a new group to bond, conduct a brief icebreaker or team-building activity at the beginning of the meeting.**

- **Assess special needs in advance.** Make arrangements to meet those needs. An association whose president required wheelchair access faced a crisis on two occasions that could have been avoided. When the group arrived at a historic hotel, there were no sleeping rooms on the first floor. There was a fire in the hotel at 5:00 a.m. Although in the end, the president was safe, there was grave concern because no one in the group knew his room number or his whereabouts. He had taken an elevator from his second floor room to safety. The same group went to a restaurant for a group dinner and found that their reservations were for a room on the second floor with no elevator access. Asking a few questions in advance would have prevented these situations.

- **Older volunteers may be hearing impaired, especially when there is background noise.** Ask people to speak loudly and clearly so everyone can hear. Keep secondary conversations to a minimum.

- **Avoid the use of true red and green markers to accommodate volunteers who are colorblind.**

- **Provide refreshments to make the work more pleasant for your volunteers.** Provide light meals after work and at meal times. Include a variety of foods and beverages. Provide healthful alternatives to high-fat and high-calorie foods and beverages. Provide diet and regular colas and bottled water for breakfast, too. Offer vegetarian meal options.

- **Avoid alcoholic beverages during meetings and work sessions.** Serving alcoholic beverages depends on the accepted practice of your organization. Check with your legal counsel to determine whether or not the association could be held responsible for accidents involving drinking and driving if alcohol is served at meetings.

- **When possible, hold multi-day meetings at sites with health clubs, running and bicycle trails, and other options for volunteers who want to maintain their daily routines.**

- **When possible, let members of the group determine the dates, places, and times of future meetings that are best for them.**

- **Provide an area for play or study for school-age children, such as a study/reading area, art materials, quiet toys, and/or a computer.** This encourages working parents to volunteer in the evenings or on Saturdays without having to be away from their children or in-curring additional childcare expenses.

Ensure that each volunteer successfully completes the assigned task and walks away with a feeling of well-being, as well as a positive image of the association as a result of the experience. If they do, they are more likely to continue to volunteer.

> 10. A volunteer needs follow-up to see that the task is completed.

The Need

Volunteer leaders frequently come from the business world and bring business models to their organizations. It is important to remember that volunteers are not employees and cannot be treated as such. Even the best and most reliable volunteers need follow-up to bring closure to the commitment. If you do not follow up, the message is communicated that the assignment was busywork and not valuable. If you have met volunteers' needs one through nine, follow up will be easy.

How to Meet the Need

- **Volunteers are colleagues and partners, not employees or subordinates.** Treating them as equals instead of someone who works for you will get better results.

- **Monitor — don't hover.** If you have provided clear direction up front, during the task you need only to monitor progress and ensure that the work is being done. Monitor new volunteers closely until they have proven themselves.

- **Most importantly, get out of the way.**

- **As the team leader, don't allow yourself to get bogged down doing the work.** Your job as the leader of your volunteer team is to monitor and troubleshoot throughout the project. Even if it seems easier to do the work yourself, your job is to coordinate many people doing specific tasks. Involving as many members as possible is a critical element to developing future volunteer leaders.

• Become a coach or cheerleader when it's needed to keep the project moving.

• Praise publicly and criticize privately. Your volunteers have given generously of their talents and time; nothing will chase them away faster than public humiliation.

• If a volunteer is not working out, the responsibility for finding out why and addressing the reasons lies with you, the team leader, not the volunteer. Address the issue as soon as it comes to your attention. Contact the unsatisfactory volunteer first via telephone, then e-mail, and then regular mail. If needed, schedule a face-to-face meeting. Attempt to find out the reasons why things are not working out. In some cases the reason for nonperformance is not easy to understand. Solicit ideas from the volunteer about why it's not working. Ask what they need from you or others in the organization in order to perform the task. Try to provide what they tell you they need.

• Review the 12 basic needs to see if you can better meet the volunteer's needs. Reassigning the volunteer to another task that's a better match for him or her may work, or simply providing more direction or training may also work.

• In some cases, another volunteer may be the problem. If you find a disruptive volunteer in your group, you may have to re-assign him or her to a task that can be done more independently. If you have assigned an ending time to each volunteer task, you will be able to thank him or her and make certain that he or she is not asked to work in a similar situation again.

• In other cases, events happen that prevent volunteers from keeping their commitments — changes in employment, additional work or family responsibilities, illnesses and death, or just overload. They may not say anything because they feel bad that they cannot keep their commitment to you and they really hope the situation will change. If this has happened, let them know that you understand their situation, thank them, and release them from their commitment. Leave the door open for future involvement when the situation changes.

When a Volunteer Doesn't Perform

It is inevitable that at some point in your experience of managing volunteers, you will have to face the problem of nonperformance. Most volunteer leaders and staff are not willing to confront the problem of nonperformance of volunteers. Since volunteers are not on the payroll and the relationship is not between an employee and supervisor, the situation is especially sensitive. The most effective way to address the question of performance is to attempt to have experienced volunteer project team leaders for each major project. Assigning an ending time to each task will also minimize the times that problems occur. Here are some helpful tips for addressing nonperformance by a volunteer:

- **Remember that volunteers won't always work out, but as the project team leader, it's your responsibility to address the issue so that others who are working on the project don't suffer.**

- **It is best if a volunteer leader rather than a staff person addresses a volunteer's nonperformance.** In cases where a staff person is serving as the project team leader and working directly with the volunteers, it is appropriate for the staff person to involve the volunteer leaders if the problem continues to exist.

- **Yes, you can fire a volunteer if all of your attempts to get the volunteer back on track have failed.** Moreover, it's your responsibility to do so. If you see that the volunteer is unable to complete a task and there is nothing more you can do, it's appropriate to give him or her permission to step aside and for you to find a replacement.

• **If it comes to this, it is best if the notification comes from the volunteer project team leader or volunteer leaders.** Some leaders will elect to call the volunteer while others will meet with him or her face-to-face. They may choose to send a written notice to the volunteer. The letter in Example 10 from the project team leader on page 65, and the letter in Example 11 from the association president on page 66 are appropriate for members who are not performing after all efforts to address the problem have been made. The contents of these sample letters may be adapted for use in a phone call or meeting.

(letterhead)

Joan Greenberg
1234 Main Street
Maryville, GA 44444

Dear Joan,

I was very pleased that you agreed to help judge the awards program this year. I understand that [changes in your family responsibilities, your new job/promotion, your relocation, other elected positions, etc.] have required you to re-order your priorities. Because judging is such a critical element of the awards program, I must replace you on the panel of judges. Although I will miss working with you, I certainly understand why you have not been able to keep your commitment to serve as a judge this year.

Thank you for your willingness to volunteer for the Maryville Chapter of XYZ Association. The time and talent of many member volunteers make it possible for us to carry on our awards programs. Hopefully you will be able to serve as a judge or in a similar capacity if your situation changes.

Good luck on [refer to reason above] and again, thank you.

Sincerely,

Carlos

Carlos Hernandez
Project Team Leader, Awards Program
Maryville Chapter of XYZ Association

Example 10

(letterhead)

Joan Greenberg
1234 Main Street
Maryville, GA 44444

Dear Joan:

The Executive Committee met on Tuesday, May 3, at which time they reviewed current membership of the board of directors.

The consensus of the committee was that since you were unable to fulfill the requirements of the board position due to job and time constraints, we must appoint a new board member to fulfill the position's requirements.

We appreciate your interest in volunteering for the association and understand that sometimes time doesn't allow for these additional responsibilities. In fairness to the rest of the board, we need to replace you with someone who can commit the time to actively participate in board activities. Hopefully you will be able to serve our chapter again if your situation changes.

Please accept our thanks and best wishes!

Sincerely,

Maurie

Maurice Blackwell
President
Maryville Chapter of XYZ Association

Example 11

Your job as a volunteer officer, board member, committee or task force chair, project or work team leader is not to do the work yourself, but to get results through your volunteer team. By monitoring your teams' progress, you demonstrate that their contribution is important and you ensure that the work is getting done properly.

> *11. A volunteer needs an opportunity to provide feedback when the task is finished.*

The Need

Asking for feedback from volunteers gives them the opportunity to share their experiences and provide suggestions for how the experience and the results can be improved. Even the best plans will not be flawless, but without asking the volunteer for feedback you might never know about all the problems that have occurred. You may lose volunteers over incidents that can be prevented in the future.

How to Meet the Need

Provide an Opportunity for Volunteers to Evaluate the Experience

- **When you are wrapping up the project, get feedback from all the volunteers.** Ask how things went and what would have made their experiences better.

- **In some cases, a follow-up phone call or e-mail from the project team leader is all that is needed so the volunteer has the opportunity to be heard.** For larger projects, a short and simple written summary is more helpful. The sample cover note in Example 12 on page 69 and the Volunteer Project Evaluation form in Example 13 on page 70 may be used for written feedback or adapted for use in a telephone call.

Date: December 1
To: Sylvia White
From: Martin Long, Director of Membership
Re: Volunteer Project Evaluation

Won't you take a minute to give me some feedback on your recent volunteer experience? It will help me maximize the contributions of volunteers in the future and make their experiences as pleasant as possible. Simply complete and return the enclosed Volunteer Project Evaluation form in the envelope provided, or fax it to me at the number at the bottom of the form.

Thank you,

Martin

Example 12

Volunteer Project Evaluation *

Project description: 1999 Annual Conference

On the scale of 0 to 5 where 0 is "not at all satisfied" and 5 is "extremely satisfied," please rate your satisfaction with the following elements of your volunteer experience by circling a number from 0 to 5. The higher the number, the more satisfied you are with the experience.

Not at all satisfied   Extremely satisfied

Overall satisfaction with your experience

0   1   2   3   4   5

Amount of follow-up and support received from your team leader

0   1   2   3   4   5

Quality of meetings and work sessions (Time well spent, adequate preparation, pleasant environment)

0   1   2   3   4   5

Degree to which everything you needed to complete the task was provided (Tools, information, training)

0   1   2   3   4   5

Degree to which commitments made to you were kept

0   1   2   3   4   5

Did you experience any problems or difficulties that we need to address in order to make your future volunteer experience better? (Please describe. Attach additional page if needed.)

If you would like to discuss your experience further, please write your name and phone number below and I will call you.

Name: _____

Telephone: (_____)_____

Return in the enclosed envelope, or fax to 888-555-4444. Thank you.

Example 13

---

*Information for downloading a master copy of this form from the Internet is located on the last page of this book.

Require a Written Summary Report from the Project Team Leader

All too often volunteers must unnecessarily start a project from scratch because the previous project team leader did not complete a summary report and file it with the association. Ensuring that a report is filed at the end of each project and handed to the next team leader will save valuable time and resources.

- **Request a final report that summarizes the completed project.** This provides a history for the team that will pick up the project the next time.

- **Provide a reporting form.** Ask that it be returned within 30 days after the end of the project.

- **Collect project planning worksheets, tracking forms, and volunteer project evaluations as a part of the report.**

- **Solicit interest in subsequent involvement.** Recommend volunteers to next year's project coordinators. A section may be added to the Volunteer Project Evaluation form to accomplish this task, but it is better if you identify the best volunteers and talk to them before the project ends.

- **Make the completed report the admission ticket to a thank you event for volunteers.**

- **Follow up to collect reports that are not turned in by the deadline.** Pass the completed report to your staff coordinator or directly to the new team to help them get started. When the next team of volunteers takes over, they won't have to start from scratch.

- **Take this opportunity to evaluate the performance of volunteers.** Develop a list of rising stars. Groom the most talented and committed volunteers and encourage them to move into positions with more responsibilities and eventually to become leaders.

> 12. A volunteer needs appreciation, recognition, and rewards that match the reasons for volunteering.

The Need

This need is one of the easiest and least expensive to meet, yet it is frequently overlooked. No matter how small the contribution, each volunteer deserves acknowledgement that what he or she did was of value and greatly appreciated.

How to Meet the Need

- **When volunteers complete the task or fulfill their commitment of time, thank them and let them go.**

- **Thank each volunteer personally.** A simple note handwritten on your organization's thank-you notes sent immediately after the project is completed is the most basic and effective thank you.

- **Track volunteers' contributions so you can be specific with your praise and recognition.** Be precise about the time, date, and nature of the individual's contribution and how it related to the success of the project. Make sure each volunteer knows that his or her personal assistance was important and appreciated.

- **Avoid sales incentive and reward models when working with volunteers.** You'll get better results when you reward and recognize everyone who contributed rather than offering contests that reward only top producers. Awarding a "top producer" who was responsible for 15% of your goal may slight the rest of the group, who, after all, are responsible for the other 85% of the results.

- **Don't address thank you notes to "Dear Volunteers."** Take the time to acknowledge each individual contribution.

- **Hand write or print a personalized note or create a personalized e-mail.** Thank individuals on a one-to-one basis.

- **One chapter president surprised her new board with chocolates and champagne after their first meeting.** She also wrote board members a personalized thank you note for giving of their valuable time to attend an all-day board orientation. The following sample thank you note in Example 14 was placed in an association's on-line discussion group. It does not thank each volunteer personally. The examples in Example 15 and 16 on pages 74-75 thank a volunteer for a specific contribution.

Dear Volunteers,

    As many of you know, I was the Volunteer Coordinator at our recent XYZ conference. I want to send a very public thank you to everyone who heeded my pleas to volunteer. Your work makes the conference go smoothly and cheerfully, and saves my blood pressure. Thanks, again!

Jennifer Brown
Conference Coordinator

Example 14

(notecard)

Dear Bill,

Thank you! Thank you! Thank you!

Thank you for working at the registration desk Tuesday afternoon during our Annual Education Conference. Your contribution was very important in ensuring that our conference was a success. I sincerely appreciate your responding to my request for your help. The conference would not have been the same without your giving your time. I hope we get an opportunity to work together again soon.

Again, thank you.

Sincerely,

Pat

Pat Martinson
Project Team Leader, Conference Registration
Moline Chapter of XYZ Association

Example 15

(notecard)

Dear Ellen,

Thank you for all the time and energy you devoted to the host committee. I appreciated being able to count on you to introduce the speaker at Wednesday's luncheon. You are a superb colleague and I look forward to working with you again in the future.

Most sincerely,

Judy

Judith Melons
Project Team Leader, Host Committee
Chicago Chapter of XYZ Association

Example 16

Follow up with recognition. The examples below are appropriate for some of the most common motives for volunteering reviewed earlier in this chapter.

Leadership/Power/Prestige

Give them a job with increased authority and an important title. Name an event or scholarship after them. Make a donation in their name. Introduce them to important people such as well-known speakers or officers from the higher levels of your organization.

Recognition

Give them visibility during the project by listing their names in your newsletters, programs, and news releases.

Make them the subject of feature articles on topics in their areas of their expertise. Use rewards and recognition that give them visibility when the project is completed. Present them with a plaque or framed certificate of appreciation at a banquet, send a letter of praise to their employer, deliver a news release to a newsletter at their place of employment, or nominate them for an award.

Affiliation/Socialization

Honor this group with a volunteer banquet. Reward them with their name and photo in your newsletter, a note of thanks, a party, a personalized gift, or a thank you letter from the president or team leader.

Social

Celebrate the completion of the project with a party or social event. Many organizations hold an annual volunteer appreciation day during National Volunteer Week in April.

Creativity/Self-Expression

This group will enjoy the most unique recognition you can think of — a framed photograph of them with the finished project, a skit at an appreciation event, or an original drawing or poem.

No one ever has complained about being praised too much.

CHAPTER FOUR

Planning for Leadership Succession

As was pointed out earlier in this book, the best place to get new volunteers is at the chapter level. However, a long-term objective is to identify and mentor the best volunteers to become tomorrow's leaders and officers of the chapter and eventually at progressively higher levels of the organization — district, regional, state, national, and international. This takes careful planning and coordination by the volunteer leaders and staff at each level.

Stages of Volunteer Development

With proper mentoring and direction, volunteers pass through four stages of development from new volunteer to seasoned volunteers — new volunteers, work team leaders, project team leaders, and finally leaders/officers. Each stage is important if volunteers are to be ready for the tasks and responsibilities of the stage that follows. Progression through these stages occurs at different time intervals.

Keep in mind that typically the number of volunteers who continue from one stage to the next becomes progressively smaller so that approximately five percent become leaders and officers. The rest drop out or choose to stay at a level of development.

- **Recruit as many volunteers as possible for at least one task during each year.**

- **A number of volunteers will be interested in assuming more responsibility and learning new skills.** Identify these individuals early and move them into positions with more responsibility, new challenges, and valuable rewards.

- **The time to find replacements for key volunteer leaders is at the beginning of a project.** Identify a volunteer "understudy" for each key position.

- **Identify and groom up-and-coming leaders early.** With careful mentoring and training provided by the current volunteer leader, individuals who have leadership potential will be ready to step into leadership positions when needed. As your most motivated and experienced volunteers move into positions of more responsibility, they form a larger and more experienced pool of project leaders from which to draw volunteer leaders and officers. This results in better standing-committee chairpersons, board members, and eventually officers. See the stages of volunteer development in Figure 2 on the following page.

Building a Leadership Cadre for Every Level of Your Organization

Continually feeding new volunteers into a development path and moving them along as they mature ensures a pool of experienced volunteers ready to fill vacancies in leadership positions at all levels of the organization.

- **Develop a succession plan for your organization.** Ensure that the best volunteers are guided on the path to becoming volunteer leaders and officers.

- **The volunteer leaders and officers at the closest-to-home chapter level form a pool of experienced volunteers for the next level, the district/region.** In turn, the district/region volunteer leaders form a pool from which the state/district level draws. In turn state/district leaders and officers form a pool for the national/regional level, and so on.

- **Solicit volunteers for each level from the appropriate pool.** If yours is a chapter-level organization, recruit volunteers from your total chapter membership. If yours is the district or region-level organization that has chapters, recruit volunteers from the volunteer leaders and officers from all of your chapters and not from the membership at large. If your group is the state-level organization that has district or regional-level

Stages of Volunteer Development

New Volunteers	Work Team Leaders	Project Team Leaders	Leaders/Officers
Perform single, low-risk tasks of short duration	Proven to be dependable	Demonstrated ability to take on larger and higher risk tasks	Top 5% of members who are leaders/officers at each level
Require support, careful monitoring, and close evaluation	Successfully completed one or more tasks of longer duration	Capable of coordinating multiple work teams	Form the pool from which the next level of the organization recruits volunteers
Top performers take on more complex and longer-term tasks	Committed to organization and goals	Some choose to stay at this stage	Some choose to stay at this stage
Some choose to stay at this stage	Demonstrated ability and interest in leading groups	Some drop out	Some drop out
Some drop out	Interested in becoming more involved	Grooming begins for future leaders/officers at same level of organization	Some become leaders/officers of next level
Top performers become work team leaders	Willing to recruit and manage their own work teams		
	Some choose to stay at this stage		
	Some drop out		
	Top performers become understudies to become project team leaders		

Figure 2

affiliates, recruit volunteers from the volunteer leaders in all of the district/region affiliates, and so on. See Figure 3 below.

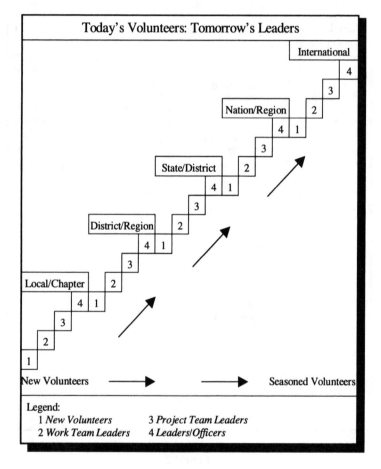

Figure 3

Models for Organizing Volunteers

Old Hierarchical Model

The traditional organizational chart model of top-down management based on a hierarchical reporting structure does not accommodate the need to organize volunteers into work teams of colleagues, each responsible for one or more manageable pieces of the total project. The following are characteristics of this traditional structure:

- **The organizational chart places the Chief Elected Officer at the top and volunteers at the bottom.**

- **The path from new volunteer to leader/officer may take from five to seven years or more and may require a member to occupy virtually every position along the way.** When a shortage of volunteers occurs, new volunteers are moved into leadership positions before they are prepared for the roles.

- **Volunteer leaders serve as managers instead of coaches and work *over* rather than *with* or *beside* volunteers.**

- **Longevity is rewarded with re-election and reappointment.**

- **Standing committees carry out most of the activities in long-term assignments.** There are few short-term assignments for volunteers.

- **Committee chairpersons may remain in positions indefinitely or be re-elected for an unlimited number of terms.**

- **Committee members report to committee chairs and are expected to attend all committee meetings.**

- **Related functions of a program or activity are not always coordinated.** Figure 4 on the following page shows the traditional hierarchical structure.

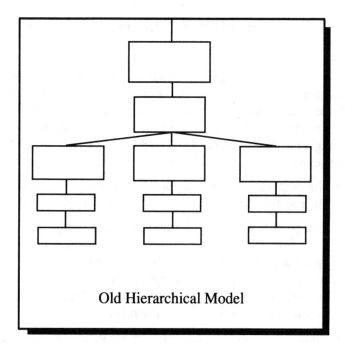

Figure 4

New Project Team Model

A new structural model is emerging that accommodates volunteers' need for ad hoc assignments that are of short duration. It recognizes that not all volunteers want to eventually become officers. The following are characteristics of the new project team model:

- Tasks are divided into logical groupings and assigned to teams of volunteers; the more team members, the less work for each person.

- Task forces and assignments offer opportunities for volunteers to make short term commitments.

- Team leaders coordinate project activities and serve as coaches to their teams.

- **Team members divide up the assigned tasks.** They work independently to complete their component of the project, either alone or with their own work teams.

- **Each project team leader has an understudy/trainee.** He or she will be ready to take over as leader.

- **For larger projects, the project team leaders meet regularly to coordinate the activities of their teams.**

- **If volunteers do not want to be project leaders, they are encouraged to continue at the team level.**

- **As volunteers mature and show interest, they are trained to create a volunteer work team of their own and given larger and higher-risk projects.**

- **When a task is completed, the team is dissolved.** Figure 5 below shows the new project team model.

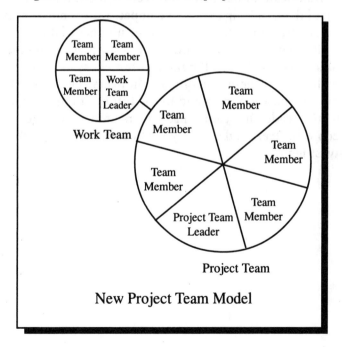

New Project Team Model

Figure 5

Reaping Long-Term Benefits of Meeting Volunteers' Needs

Meeting volunteers' needs creates a win-win situation. It is probably obvious that volunteers benefit when you understand and meet their needs. In reality, your organization wins, too.

By its very nature, your membership organization must have meaningful volunteer activity to survive. Volunteering builds commitment and loyalty to your organization. Because members often judge the value of membership by their experience at the local level, the best place to get members involved is at the closest-to-home level. Members who actively participate are more satisfied and are more likely to renew their memberships. This means more members, volunteers, and dollars for the association.

American adults still volunteer — more than 93 million of them. It is up to you to compete for the most skilled and talented volunteers with a large number of other non-profit organizations and competing priorities. If you meet volunteers' needs, you'll build a volunteer system that will result in more, better-qualified volunteers at every level of your organization, now and in the future. It's up to you to create a leadership cadre that understands how to get and keep volunteers and ensure your future. There is no better investment.

CHAPTER FIVE
Case Studies

Case Studies

The following cases are true stories. Although they may seem to be exaggerated to emphasize the difference between the right and wrong way to work with volunteers, I can assure you no embellishment was used. Names, locations, and details that would identify the individuals or organizations have been changed, and the identities of the organizations have been omitted.

Annual Conference

XYZ Baltimore is a local association affiliated with XYZ National. Although the two organizations share a common mission, they are organized as two separate nonprofit corporations. Individuals may be members of one or both organizations so there is a large crossover in membership. XYZ Baltimore was asked to be the local host for the national association's annual convention scheduled for July.

Several months before the convention, XYZ Baltimore named its president-elect, Richard Welch, to chair the host committee. Richard scheduled the initial meeting of the group and sent a letter to all members, inviting anyone interested in being on the committee to attend.

One local volunteer leader, Margaret Baker, who had been a member of both XYZ Baltimore and XYZ National for nine years, decided to volunteer for the committee. She had recently completed a three-year term on the board of directors and had chaired several key committees over the years.

The meeting was scheduled for 3:00 p.m. on a weekday afternoon in a city 60 miles away. Margaret scheduled her work so that she had plenty of time to arrive on time. The notice of the meeting contained the address of the meeting and information on public transportation within the city, but no information on the location or cost of parking. When she approached the meeting place, she found herself in a maze of one-way streets, street construction projects, and no street parking. She found two parking garages within walking distance of the meeting but both were full. She finally found a parking garage with space and a hefty parking fee.

Margaret arrived at the meeting with no time to spare. The room was small and crowded. There were soft drinks and cookies on a table in the corner, but chairs already occupied blocked access to it. Although several members were new volunteers, no one wore nametags. Margaret recognized most people in the group of about 35 members. Like her, many had commuted for more than an hour and paid hefty parking fees in order to attend the meeting. There was no one from XYZ National present.

Richard called the meeting to order 15 minutes after the advertised starting time. With no evidence of an agenda, Richard began the meeting with a round of self-introductions. He thanked everyone for attending and then proceeded to talk about the conference in general — the dates, location, how many attendees were expected, and other items included in pre-conference materials XYZ National members had already received. Richard did not say anything about what was expected of members of the committee or how much time each would be asked to work. There was no mention of the costs involved or who would pay for parking or meals. Margaret kept wondering when Richard would talk about the details of the assignment, but the meeting continued with no specific plans for the committee. No one in the group asked for details. After 90 minutes, the meeting adjourned with no clear charge for what the host committee was to do. Margaret returned home in the middle of rush hour traffic with no more understanding of her committee responsibility than when she had started. The wasted afternoon cost her five hours of time and $12 for parking.

Being the dedicated member that she was, Margaret did not quit. When she received the notice for the next meeting she found that it was scheduled for the Friday afternoon that she was planning to leave town for the Memorial Day weekend. She adjusted her travel plans so she could attend the meeting.

The three-day weekend added to the travel time for her 60-mile commute and to the traffic within the city. This time Margaret knew where parking garages were located and how much she would have to pay for parking.

The second meeting was similar to the first. Again there was no evidence of an agenda. There were members present who were not at the first meeting, yet there were no introductions or nametags. Much of the information from the first meeting was repeated at this one. The only new information was provided when Chairperson Richard read the names of members who had been pre-assigned to a handful of subcommittees. Margaret had been assigned to the publicity subcommittee along with two other members of the committee. Barbara Santos was designated as chairperson of the subcommittee. Publicity was an area in which Margaret had expertise but little interest. Offered no alternatives, she agreed to the assignment without objection. The meeting adjourned with little interaction among members of the group and no questions were asked.

The publicity subcommittee was given no charge. Although they were frustrated, they met to develop a plan of activities for promoting the conference locally. They developed a list of 10 activities that could be carried out in conjunction with a neighboring association to encourage attendance of area members. They identified resources and estimated the cost of each activity. Chairperson Barbara Santos submitted their suggestions in writing to Richard, the committee chair, but never heard about them again or saw any evidence that they were used. The subcommittee did not meet again.

Shortly before the convention, committee members received a letter asking them to volunteer as much time as they could during the convention. Feeling that she had not yet contributed anything to the project, Margaret signed up for the afternoon of the first day of registration. There was no indication of what she would be doing during the afternoon shift, but she signed up anyway. Since she had to drive more than an hour each way, she also volunteered to work from 5:00 to 7:00 p.m. the same evening to cut down on the need for a second trip. During the evening she would help at an event to be held at a site in another part of the city.

Margaret received a voice-mail message asking her to report to the host meeting room at the convention center at 11:00 a.m. on the day she had selected. She expected that she would be given instructions and a specific assignment by a coordinator. When she reported to the assigned room at the agreed time, it was empty. There were no other volunteers, no staff, no food or beverages, no nametags or list of other volunteers scheduled to work that day, and no signs or instructions in sight. She had not been provided with the names of a coordinator or other members who were volunteering that day.

After waiting a while, she walked to the registration area. As she passed a special registration table for premier conference attendees, a colleague, Greg Monahan, asked her to help him. It was almost noon, and he had been working since early morning when registration began, without help and with no one to relieve him for a break. Greg gave brief instructions on how he had handled registration and answered questions based on his experiences from that morning. No one had told him who the premier registrants were. Like Margaret, he had received no training or written instructions for his task.

Shortly after she started working, Greg asked Margaret if she would stay so he could get some lunch. There was no food in the host meeting room or food service in the convention center that day, so he left the convention center in search of something to eat.

It was quite busy at the table, with a lot of work for one person to handle. When a registrant asked a question Margaret couldn't answer, there was no one to turn to for an answer. Several times people approached the premier table to register, assuming that it was for VIPs and they were the VIPs. They were most unhappy when Margaret did not have their registration packets and sent them to the regular tables to stand in line. They asked who the "premier" registrants were and Margaret did not know. She later found out that they were the attendees who had registered by an early deadline.

When Greg returned from lunch, he picked up his belongings and left, assuming that his shift was over. Margaret continued to work alone until 3 p.m. when another volunteer wandered past the registration table. As Greg had done, she recognized the opportunity to get someone to take over for her. Margaret was now free for two hours before her evening commitment. She too wandered outside the convention center in search of lunch.

Shortly before 5 p.m., Margaret drove to her evening assignment in another area of the city. This time she found two-hour metered parking on the street nearby. When she reported to the assigned location, she found a coordinator from a special events company in charge. When the group of volunteers assembled, they were given matching jackets and explicit instructions on where they were to stand and what they were to do. Margaret was assigned to welcome conference attendees as they arrived on buses and guide them to the next volunteers who would guide them to the event location.

Fifteen minutes after the group of volunteers had assembled for instructions and reported to their stations, buses of attendees began to arrive. Everything went as planned, and Margaret did exactly what she committed to do. All buses had arrived and the attendees were inside by 7 p.m. She was ready to give her association an A+ for how it handled the volunteers during the evening assignment and forgive them for not being more considerate during the day. After standing for nearly eight hours and paying for her own parking and lunch, she felt that she had more than fulfilled her commitment and had contributed to the success of the conference. She was preparing to leave when she heard someone calling her name. It was the same coordinator, who was giving her another assignment that was totally unrelated to the tasks she had committed to and completed. Margaret found herself apologizing that she had to leave because she had prior commitments. She left feeling exhausted and frustrated from the entire experience.

In mid-September, Margaret received a handwritten note from the host committee chairperson of XYZ Baltimore, Richard Welch. It was written on his company's letterhead and consisted of two sentences thanking her for her time and energy and telling her that he was looking forward to working with her in the future. It did not mention the subcommittee work or the events of the day she had worked at the conference.

Several months later, Margaret received a small package from XYZ National. It contained a letter and a beautiful silver business card holder engraved with the association's logo. Her immediate response was that it was a very thoughtful and useful gift, but her bubble soon burst when she read the letter. After thanking her for helping with the convention, it said the business card holders were *leftovers* from the gifts given to the convention attendees and were being sent to members of the host committee.

More than two years have passed since these events occurred. Margaret has not volunteered for any more tasks. Although she had made four trips of two hours or more each, paid for parking and her meals, and worked the hours she committed to, no one has asked her to volunteer for this organization again.

Were This Volunteer's Needs Met?

How well did XYZ Baltimore meet Margaret's needs as a volunteer? Review the needs in items 1–12 in Column 1 below. Indicate whether the organization met each need by checking the box in Column 2 if "yes," Column 3 if "partially," or Column 4 if "no." Repeat for XYZ National.

12 Basic Needs of Every Volunteer			
(1)	(2)	(3)	(4)
	Yes	Partially	No
1. A specific manageable task with a beginning and an end	☐	☐	☐
2. A task that matches interests and reasons for volunteering	☐	☐	☐
3. A good reason for doing the task	☐	☐	☐
4. Written instructions	☐	☐	☐
5. A reasonable deadline for completing task	☐	☐	☐
6. Freedom to complete task *when* and *where* it is most convenient for the volunteer	☐	☐	☐
7. Everything necessary to complete the task without interruption	☐	☐	☐
8. Adequate training	☐	☐	☐
9. A safe, comfortable, and friendly working environment	☐	☐	☐
10. Follow-up to see that the task is completed	☐	☐	☐
11. An opportunity to provide feedback when the task is finished	☐	☐	☐
12. Appreciation, recognition, and rewards that match the reasons for volunteering	☐	☐	☐

Figure 6

The Score: An Analysis

Compare your ratings with the following analysis which summarizes what the associations did to meet Margaret's needs and suggestions for what they could have done to make the experience better. In summary, Margaret had the same needs as all volunteers. Yet, a quick review of the list of the 12 basic needs that volunteers share reveals that not all of these needs were met.

> 1. A specific manageable task with a beginning and an end.
>   ❑ Yes   ❑ Partially   ☒ No

- The role of the local host committee did not appear to be defined for the local board, the host committee chair, the host committee, or the subcommittee.

- Assignments left a lot of room for differing expectations. Yet, no one asked questions that would have clarified what was expected.

- When volunteers showed up to work, there was no volunteer or staff coordinator to assign them to a specific task or provide what they needed to successfully complete that task.

- Meetings had a beginning time but no predetermined ending time.

- Margaret was asked to report at a specific time the day of registration but was given no specific ending time.

- At the evening event, the time block was specific but the task was not defined until Margaret arrived. At the end of the negotiated two-hour block and completion of the task, the event coordinator attempted to assign another task without first negotiating with Margaret for more time.

- Each year a different XYZ local is host for the conference. Defining the role of the local host committee and determining who was going to provide what would have eliminated many problems. More discussion with the convention planners from XYZ National would have clarified the host committee's role.

- Advance planning would have helped the host committee chairperson break the workload into specific tasks with beginning and ending times before putting out the call for volunteers.

- Assigning one of the host committee members to be volunteer coordinator on site at the convention center would have prevented many problems.

---

2. A task that matches interests and reasons for volunteering.

☐ Yes   ☐ Partially   ☒ No

- Assignments to the subcommittees were made without any discussion with individual volunteers.

- The committee chair, Richard, assumed that Margaret was interested in working in an area in which she had expertise because she was employed in that area.

- More one-to-one communication with the committee members after the first meeting would have made it easy to match interests with tasks.

---

3. A good reason for doing the task.

☐ Yes   ☐ Partially   ☒ No

- XYZ National did not specify what it needed from XYZ Baltimore before that group formed its host committee, so reasons for the tasks were not clear.

- There was no apparent reason for having a subcommittee for publicity. No charge was given to the group, and their suggestions were not acknowledged or used.

- It would have helped if XYZ Baltimore had been given a list of what was expected from the committee up front. Designating specific expectations, such as supplying volunteers to work registration tables, take tickets, and work at the information desk, would have provided guidance to the XYZ Baltimore host committee chairperson early in the formation of the committee. It would have prevented volunteers from wasting time and money attending meetings.

---

4. Written instructions.

☐ Yes   ☐ Partially   ☒ No

- There were no written instructions of any kind.

- Volunteers were only told when and where meetings were held and when to report at the convention center once they had signed up for shifts.

- There were no instructions for how to work registration, no schedule of who was working when, and no names of whom to go to with questions.

---

5. A reasonable deadline for completing the task.
☒ Yes   ☐ Partially   ☐ No

- The deadline was dictated by the event.

- The convention was held on specific days and the activities were conducted within specific time blocks.

---

6. Freedom to complete a task *when* and *where* it is most convenient for the volunteer.

   ❑ Yes   ☒ Partially   ❑ No

- Meetings were held even when there was no specific agenda item that required group interaction, decision making, or discussion.

- There was not much flexibility for volunteers to work at home or in their offices because of the nature of the event. The tasks at the convention had to be performed on site.

- Subcommittee work could have been done by a telephone conference call.

---

7. Everything necessary to complete the task without interruption.

   ❑ Yes   ☒ Partially   ❑ No

- In the case of registration, little or no information about the premier desk was provided to the volunteers.

- The task at the special event did not require any special skills, information, or training other than what was given in the briefing when the volunteers reported.

8. Adequate training.

    ❑ Yes   ❎ Partially   ❑ No

- The most serious oversight was in not training the host committee chairperson.
- There was no training or orientation for working registration.
- An orientation and clear instructions were provided for the volunteers who were welcoming and ushering conference attendees at the off-site event.

9. A safe, comfortable, and friendly working environment.

    ❑ Yes   ❑ Partially   ❎ No

- The meeting notices did not include information on parking or a map.
- Food was provided at the committee meeting but was not accessible.
- The host committee room at the convention room did not have food or beverages even though volunteers were working on-site during normal lunch and dinner hours. Volunteers were not told they would have to pay for their own meals.
- Volunteers did not have nametags.
- Parking was expensive and not discussed ahead of time. Volunteers were expected to pay for their own parking, and it was assumed that the volunteers knew this without discussing it up front.

- Volunteers were left to introduce themselves to one another. A volunteer coordinator on site would have helped make the volunteers more comfortable, especially new volunteers.

> 10. Follow-up to see that the task is completed.
> ☐ Yes   ☐ Partially   ☒ No

- There was no follow-up to see that the volunteers arrived at the appointed time the day of the conference.
- There was no indication that anyone was coordinating volunteer efforts on site. Volunteers would have benefited from having a coordinator on site at all times to provide support and answer questions. This would have been a good way to use some of the host committee members.

> 11. An opportunity to provide feedback when the task is finished.
> ☐ Yes   ☐ Partially   ☒ No

- Perhaps the most troubling aspect of this entire story is that no one in the host organization or the national association ever knew what happened. No one ever asked. Margaret was not given an opportunity to provide feedback about her experience.
- It is not known if the host committee chairperson or association staff wrote a report for the national association, but if they did, it would not have included

suggestions for how to make the volunteer experience more valuable and satisfying.

12. Appreciation, recognition, and rewards that match the reasons for volunteering.

  ❑ Yes   ☒ Partially   ❑ No

- No one asked Margaret about her reasons for volunteering.

- Ironically, the handwritten note was appropriate for Margaret because she valued the relationships developed during her volunteer activities.

- Sending each volunteer a personalized thank-you letter from XYZ National was a good idea, although it contained no mention of the specific work each volunteer had done.

- Sending silver business card holders to the volunteer host committee was a good idea, but it would have been even better if they had not been told that they were leftover gifts for convention attendees. Whether they were ordered for the host committee or leftover gifts for convention attendees, no one had to know.

On a final note, as a volunteer, Margaret could have asked for what she needed, but she did not.

Children's Hospital

Sylvia Warren had been toying with the idea of volunteering in her community for several months. Sylvia's profile was typical of the 49% of Americans who volunteer: a graduate degree, some past community volunteer experience, an interest in the cause of the organizations she was considering, within the upper income brackets, and a professional. Like many potential volunteers, she was struggling with her desire to give something back and her need to juggle numerous work, family, and social commitments.

Sylvia picked a nonprofit hospital to be the recipient of her volunteer work. One sunny Saturday in February, she walked to Children's Hospital near her home to inquire about volunteer opportunities. A receptionist who was a volunteer told her that there was a formal process for becoming a volunteer. She gave her the telephone number of the volunteer office and suggested that she call on Monday to start the process.

On Monday, Sylvia called the volunteer office. The person who answered the phone politely informed her that informational meetings for perspective volunteers were held twice a year, and the next one was scheduled for May. Sylvia's first reaction was, "Wow! May. I was expecting to start this week." The person then asked Sylvia for her name and address and promised to send a postcard confirming the time and date of the meeting.

True to their word, in April the hospital sent a card to Sylvia with details of the May meeting. She marked her calendar and scheduled her work and social events around the meeting, knowing that if she missed the date, she would be locked out until the following autumn.

The meeting was held in a packed auditorium, with the Director of Volunteer Resources, Carol Wallace, as the hostess. The meeting started on time. As Carol reviewed the evening's agenda, she said that she had also invited the directors of several local children's charities to present volunteer opportunities at their organizations.

Sylvia was struck by the fact that not only did the hospital have enough volunteers that they could limit new volunteer informational meetings to twice a year, but they had enough interested people that they could share them with other organizations.

The first item on the program was a video that portrayed what it was like to be a patient in the hospital, the mission and history of the hospital, and the role volunteers played in the organization. A series of presentations was given that followed the order and time on the agenda. Each presenter, whether a hospital representative or a representative of one of the visiting organizations, was well organized and finished within the allotted time.

Following the presentations, Carol clearly outlined what was expected of volunteers at the hospital. She pointed out that her title was Director of Volunteer Resources, which was similar to a Director of Human Resources in a corporation. It was her job to screen volunteer applicants, match applicants to the appropriate position, and turn away those who were judged not to be a good fit with the organization. The potential volunteers were told that the hospital also conducted a thorough criminal background check and medical screening of each prospective volunteer.

Carol told the group that because of the large number of volunteers working at any given time, the hospital had volunteer supervisors who were full-time paid staff at the hospital. Once "hired," the volunteers would report to one of the volunteer supervisors on duty. Volunteer supervisors trained individual volunteers, set mutually agreeable work schedules, provided the tools to accomplish the job, and did whatever else was necessary to help the new volunteers become comfortable in their new volunteer assignment. Volunteers would be expected to adhere to the schedule to which they had agreed, arrange for excused absences in advance, and call in sick when necessary instead of just not showing up. Carol explained that given the hospital's strong reliance on volunteer help, in some cases — primarily due to absenteeism — volunteers were released from their responsibilities. She delivered this list of strict expectations while simultaneously expressing her gratitude and enthusiasm for the fresh group of prospective volunteers.

Carol asked each volunteer prospect to carefully select the hospital or one of the visiting organizations in which he or she had the strongest interest. She also asked prospects to think about what type of job most interested them. For instance, if a person was not comfortable with blood, he or she would not want to be assigned to the emergency room. However, if a prospective volunteer was a retired nurse or a pre-med student seeking a close-up look at work in a hospital, he or she might want to be assigned to the emergency room. If a prospective volunteer worked with computers all day long, he or she might want to run the computer cube of the playroom. On the other hand, that same prospect may not want to get within a mile of a computer after work hours and might want to help in the art and crafts corral. In summary, Carol stated she wanted the prospects to carefully consider the areas in which they would be most comfortable making a commitment, since they were being asked to commit for a full year.

Carol then pointed out that the screening process was very involved. She acknowledged that although many prospects had started the volunteering process as far back as the previous November, it might be the coming November, one year later, before they would actually would start their assignment.

The last item on the agenda was to sign up for interviews. There were four sign-up stations, each staffed with current volunteers. Interview time slots were available from May through August on a first-come, first-served basis. Sylvia left the meeting with a clear understanding of what volunteer opportunities existed and what would be expected of her.

Once again, Sylvia carefully marked her calendar for her July interview date. Her interview with Carol was very structured and similar to a real job interview. After inquiring about Sylvia's background and prior experience, evidence of commitments, experience with children, and general interests, she listened carefully as Sylvia talked about what she wanted from the experience, what positions most interested her, and which day of the week and what time of the day best suited her. By the end of the interview, Sylvia had secured the job. Carol enthusiastically agreed with Sylvia's first choice of doing arts and crafts with the children at their bedsides. They agreed to a work schedule, training dates, and an official start date later that month. Although most volunteers worked one 90-minute block each week, Sylvia was given the option of scheduling three-hour shifts on two Saturdays each month. This option fit into her work and travel commitments.

Training consisted of three parts:

1. **A half-day group training session that addressed general issues such as:**

- What to do in case of a fire.

- What to do in case a patient has a medical emergency.

- When it was necessary to wear masks, gowns, gloves, and goggles.

- How both the physical and emotional needs of a sick child differ from those of a healthy child.

- What topics of conversation were off-limits.

A training manual was given to each participant. The session concluded with an open-book final exam.

2. **A half-day individual training session was conducted by Sylvia's volunteer supervisor. This session trained Sylvia for her specific assignment in arts and crafts, including:**

- Information on the arts and crafts that were typically available.

- Information such as where the bathrooms and cafeteria were located and where to find extra glue and crayons.

- Instructions on how to read the census report and how to fill out the post-visit report.

- Instructions on checking in and out with the volunteer supervisor on duty and the type of items to report — any supplies that were running low or items the children particularly liked.

- Special handling of patients in isolation and of transplant patients.

- Administrative details about identification cards, easy-to-read permanent name badges, and free parking passes.

3. **An orientation shift with another, more seasoned volunteer. This session provided:**

- Invaluable insight into the intangibles of how to relate to the children.

- Details about the required five-minute check-in at the beginning and end of each shift with the volunteer supervisor who was always on duty.

- Guidelines for visits with children. There was no requirement that Sylvia had to visit a minimum number of children during a shift. She was told that she could spend as much time as she wanted with each child.

Sylvia has been working for more than six months. While the staff is friendly, no formal or informal rewards or recognition are offered. She has not been asked to volunteer for additional time or tasks. She has made several contributions to the hospital without being asked to do so. She knows the children appreciate what she does and she finds the work very satisfying. She is confident that she made the right choice when she volunteered at the hospital.

Were This Volunteer's Needs Met?

How well did Children's Hospital meet Sylvia's needs as a volunteer? Review the needs listed in items 1–12 in Column 1 below. Indicate whether the hospital met each need by checking the box beside the item in Column 2 if "yes," Column 3 if "partially," or Column 4 if "no."

12 Basic Needs of Every Volunteer			
(1)	(2)	(3)	(4)
	Yes	Partially	No
1. A specific manageable task with a beginning and an end	☐	☐	☐
2. A task that matches interests and reasons for volunteering	☐	☐	☐
3. A good reason for doing the task	☐	☐	☐
4. Written instructions	☐	☐	☐
5. A reasonable deadline for completing task	☐	☐	☐
6. Freedom to complete task *when* and *where* it is most convenient for the volunteer	☐	☐	☐
7. Everything necessary to complete the task without interruption	☐	☐	☐
8. Adequate training	☐	☐	☐
9. A safe, comfortable, and friendly working environment	☐	☐	☐
10. Follow-up to see that the task is completed	☐	☐	☐
11. An opportunity to provide feedback when the task is finished	☐	☐	☐
12. Appreciation, recognition, and rewards that match the reasons for volunteering	☐	☐	☐

Figure 7

The Score: An Analysis

Compare your ratings with the following analysis that summarizes what Children's Hospital did to meet Sylvia's needs and suggestions for what they could have done to make the experience better. In summary, a quick review of the 12 needs that volunteers share reveals that they did a good job of meeting these needs.

> 1. A specific manageable task with a beginning and an end.
>   ☒ Yes   ❑ Partially   ❑ No

- Sylvia walked away from the orientation meeting with a clear understanding of what was expected and what she could expect to get from the experience before making a commitment.

- She understood that she would be committing to a three-hour block of time every other Saturday for a full year.

- The vigorous screening process made her feel she was chosen as the best person for the job, which reinforced her level of commitment.

- There was no indication that strong and committed volunteers were being tapped for more complex or longer tasks.

> 2. A task that matches interests and reasons for volunteering.
>   ☒ Yes   ❑ Partially   ❑ No

- A clear description of the available jobs and a thorough interview helped to match Sylvia to the job that best suited her interests and reasons for volunteering.

3. A good reason for doing the task.
   ☒ Yes   ❏ Partially   ❏ No

- The initial volunteer informational meeting gave a solid picture of why each of the available jobs was critical to the patients at the hospital.

4. Written instructions.
   ☒ Yes   ❏ Partially   ❏ No

- Sylvia was not only given her own copy of a written manual, but it was thoroughly reviewed at the half-day general training session.
- Although written instructions were not issued on the individual job, training was thorough and proved to be adequate.

5. A reasonable deadline for completing the task.
   ☒ Yes   ❏ Partially   ❏ No

- This job was for a block of time.
- There was no requirement that a minimum number of children must be visited; rather, Sylvia was told to spend as much time as she wanted with each child. Only the length of her shift dictated her activities.

6. Freedom to complete tasks *when* and *where* it is most convenient for the volunteer.

☒ Yes   ❏ Partially   ❏ No

- Although the nature of the volunteer activity clearly prevented the freedom for Sylvia to complete the job where it was most convenient for her, she was able to choose her work schedule from a wide range of options.

7. Everything necessary to complete the task without interruption.

☒ Yes   ❏ Partially   ❏ No

- Sylvia was given everything she needed to do her job — art supplies, a list of children to visit, and instructions on how to handle special needs children.

8. Adequate training.

☒ Yes   ❏ Partially   ❏ No

- Thorough training prepared her to do a good job in an arena that was a world away from her corporate job.

9. A safe, comfortable, and friendly working environment.

☒ Yes   ❏ Partially   ❏ No

- Sylvia's volunteer supervisor introduced her to fellow volunteers. Easy-to-read name badges were not only provided, but were a required part of the uniform. Free, convenient parking was provided — a key benefit in high-traffic urban locations.

> 10. Follow-up to see that the task is completed.
>
> ☒ Yes   ❏ Partially   ❏ No

- This assignment involved a long-term assignment in lieu of a specific task to complete. It required supervision on an ongoing basis.

- A volunteer supervisor was on duty during all shifts. Each shift began and ended with a five-minute check-in with the volunteer supervisor. The presence of a volunteer supervisor on duty provided adequate supervision. If there were no paid volunteer supervisors, an unpaid volunteer supervisor or project coordinator would have been needed to provide supervision.

- Thorough training lessened the chance that a volunteer would make innocent, well-intended mistakes. Similarly, expectations were clearly outlined in the beginning so it would be easier to enforce expectations without the volunteer feeling that he or she was being singled out if his or her work was not acceptable. This allowed volunteer supervisors to offer gentle reminders and constructive comments to volunteers without them feeling they were being singled out for criticism. By being instructed up front that it was not appropriate for a volunteer to ask patients what was wrong with them, the volunteer was less likely to innocently ask the question. In such a case, the volunteer supervisor would have to step in and correct the mistake, which under other circumstances might be interpreted as personal criticism.

> 11. An opportunity to provide feedback when the task is completed.
>
>   ❏ Yes   ☒ Partially   ❏ No

- Although Sylvia has been volunteering for more than six months, she has not been asked to evaluate her experience and make suggestions for improvement.
- A notebook was provided with forms that were to be filled out after each patient visit.
- Sylvia was also encouraged to report activities that were particularly well received by the children, any supplies that were running low, and similar items that would help the supervisor.

> 12. Appreciation, recognition, and rewards that match the reasons for volunteering.
>
>   ❏ Yes   ☒ Partially   ❏ No

- Although staff was friendly and inviting, no formal or informal rewards and recognition were offered.
- Sylvia was well matched with her work at Children's Hospital. This resulted in her feeling rewarded for her contribution.
- Sylvia knows the children appreciate what she does, and she finds the work very satisfying.

While Children's Hospital appears to be a large organization with a full-time volunteer coordinator and paid volunteer supervisors, an organization of any size could score as well with unpaid volunteers who have the experience, tools, and training they need to fill these key positions.

It is apparent that Sylvia made the right choice when she selected Children's Hospital as the recipient of her volunteer efforts. She is not only likely to become a long-term volunteer but she has also made other contributions to the hospital. A review of how well this hospital scored on meeting the 12 basic needs of volunteers makes the reason for the packed auditorium quite clear.

Appendix: Self-Evaluation Checklist

How well does your association meet your volunteers' needs?

A Self-Evaluation Checklist *			
	Yes	Some-times	No
1. Does every volunteer have a paid or unpaid supervisor/coordinator?	☐	☐	☐
2. Do you take adequate time to plan a project before contacting volunteers?	☐	☐	☐
3. Do you ask a volunteer to do a specific task with a beginning and ending time?	☐	☐	☐
4. Do you contact volunteers individually?	☐	☐	☐
5. Do you assess volunteers' interests before assigning tasks?	☐	☐	☐
6. Do you recruit members to serve in the areas that they indicated an interest in, or, if you cannot use them, explain the situation, and ask them to volunteer in another area?	☐	☐	☐
7. Do you make an effort to match volunteers' interests and tasks?	☐	☐	☐
8. Do you estimate how much time each task will take before assigning it?	☐	☐	☐
9. Do you confirm each task in writing?	☐	☐	☐
10. Do you stick to the time you asked for and let the volunteer go, or negotiate for another block of time if more time is needed?	☐	☐	☐
11. Do you set a reasonable deadline for completing each task?	☐	☐	☐
12. Do you provide written instructions for what you want?	☐	☐	☐
13. Do you provide the information, skills, and tools needed to complete the task without interruption?	☐	☐	☐
14. Do you give volunteers maximum freedom to determine how tasks will be performed?	☐	☐	☐

	Yes	Some-times	No
15. Do you give volunteers maximum freedom to decide where and when the work will be done within the constraints of the project?	☐	☐	☐
16. Do you train volunteers when the task is new or complicated?	☐	☐	☐
17. Do you provide volunteer leaders and team leaders with adequate training in how to work with volunteers?	☐	☐	☐
18. Do you provide the support and follow-up that volunteers need during projects?	☐	☐	☐
19. Do you send timely and complete meeting notices with meeting dates, times, locations, and other important information?	☐	☐	☐
20. Are meetings and work sessions well planned so time is not wasted?	☐	☐	☐
21. Are your meeting places safe, comfortable, and convenient for volunteers?	☐	☐	☐
22. Do you try to make volunteers feel welcome at meetings?	☐	☐	☐
23. Do you provide food at meetings at mealtime or if members come directly from work?	☐	☐	☐
24. Do you thank each volunteer personally for his or her individual contribution?	☐	☐	☐
25. Do you ask volunteers to evaluate their experiences and make suggestions after they have finished the work?	☐	☐	☐
26. When a project is finished, do you create a written summary report and keep it on file with your association's records?	☐	☐	☐
27. Overall, do you keep your commitments to your volunteers?	☐	☐	☐

	Yes	Some-times	No
28. Do you evaluate volunteers and pass names of rising stars to leaders?	☐	☐	☐
29. Do you identify and train an understudy for each key position so he or she is ready to take over when the need arises?	☐	☐	☐
30. Do you continually involve new volunteers and move the best volunteers into positions of more responsibility and on to the next level of the organization?	☐	☐	☐
31. Do you show volunteers that they are appreciated by giving individual recognition and rewards?	☐	☐	☐
32. Does every key volunteer leadership position have a termination date?	☐	☐	☐
Column Totals			

Scoring Self-Evaluation

If mostly "yes" responses:

A "yes" response to every item is ideal. Depending on the number of "yes" responses, you could be getting your fair share of your members' time and talents. Look at your "sometimes" and "no" responses for ways to improve your volunteer recruitment and retention efforts. Develop a plan for turning each "sometimes" and "no" response into a "yes."

If mostly "sometimes" responses:

There is room for improvement. You could do more to ensure that you are getting your share of your members' time and knowledge. Educate every staff and volunteer leader about volunteers' needs and how to meet them, using suggestions and examples in this book. If you are a frustrated volunteer and want to help your association, give them this book as a gift.

If mostly "no" responses:

You're probably experiencing a serious lack of volunteers. Your members are probably making contributions in other organizations where their needs are met. If you are not already facing a lack of leaders, you probably will be soon. If you hear yourself saying, "We need to get more people involved," it's time to start implementing what you've learned in this book. If a member gave you this book, thank him or her for the gift.

---

* Information for downloading a master copy of this form from the Internet is located on the last page of this book.

About the Author

Helen Little has provided management and marketing services to nonprofit associations in the United States for more than 20 years. *Volunteers: How to Get Them, How to Keep Them* is a compilation of wisdom drawn from her work with volunteer leaders and staff in a wide array of organizations in industries ranging from medical to forestry, accounting, and education from the local through the international level. Ms. Little brings her broad base of experience as a volunteer, volunteer leader, consultant, and staff to this book. She regularly conducts programs and retreats for volunteer leaders and staff, and her articles and columns have appeared in association publications throughout the USA.

If you would like more information on how Helen Little can help your association get and keep volunteers, visit the Panacea Press, Inc., Web site.

You may access and download master copies of the forms in this book from the Internet at:

www.panaceapress.com

Username: volunteer *[please use lower case only]*

Password: forms *[please use lower case only]*